EMOTIONAL
poverty

VOLUME 2

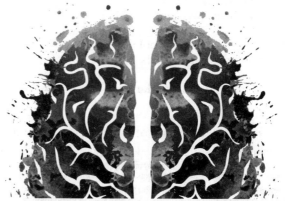

Safer Students and
Less-Stressed Teachers

Ruby K. Payne
   Emotional Poverty, Volume 2: Safer Students and Less-Stressed Teachers
   232 pages
   Bibliography: pages 201–208

   ISBN: 978-1-948244-36-7

   aha! Process, Inc.
   P.O. Box 727
   Highlands, TX 77562-0727
   (800) 424-9484 ▪ (281) 426-5300
   Fax: (281) 426-5600
   www.ahaprocess.com

Book design by Paula Nicolella
Cover design by Amy Alick Perich

Printed in White Plains, Maryland

Library of Congress Control Number: 2020941570

Permissions

Beck, Jacob. Graphic of children affected by pornography. Ever Accountable Blog, "How Porn Affects Teens [and Children]", https://everac-countable.com/blog/how-pornography-affects-teenagers-and-children. Accessed 30 March 2020. Reprinted with permission.

"Boy and His Dog," "Electroman Blue," "Heart Rhythm Patterns," and "Autonomic Nervous System" graphics from *Science of the Heart* and reprinted with permission courtesy of the HeartMath® Institute, www.heartmath.org

"Elite HRV scores" graphics and research are copyright 2020 by Elite HRV, Inc. Reprinted with permission. https://elitehrv.com

"Human learning process" graphic from *Building Expertise: Cognitive Methods for Training and Performance* (pp. 50–51), by R. C. Clark, 2008, San Francisco, CA: Pfeiffer. Copyright 2008 by John Wiley & Sons. Reprinted with permission.

"Image I.5 Traumatic Brain Injury (Brain Scan)," "Image I.6 Drug Abuse (Brain Scan)," "Image I.1 & I.2 Healthy SPECT Scan (Brain Scan)," "Image I.10.1 & I.10.2 Kent's ADD Affected Brain at Rest and Concentration (Brain Scan)," and "Underside Surface Frontal Lobe Activity (Brain Scan)" from *Change Your Brain, Change Your Life (Revised and Expanded): The Breakthrough Program for Conquering Anxiety, Depression, Obsessiveness, Lack of Focus, Anger, and Memory Problems* by Daniel G. Amen, M.D., copyright © 1998, 2015 by Daniel G. Amen, M.D. Used by permission of Harmony Books, an imprint of Random House, a division of Penguin Random House LLC. All rights reserved.

"Mirror neuron system" graphic from Rajmohan, V., & Mohandas, E. (2007). Mirror neuron system. *Indian Journal of Psychiatry, 49*(1), 66–69. Reprinted with permission. https://doi.org/10.4103/0019-5545.31522

"Narrative ecology of self" graphic from *The Coauthored Self: Family Stories and the Construction of Personal Identity* by K. McLean. Copyright 2016 by Oxford University Press. Reproduced with permission of Oxford University Press through PLSclear.

"Noise cancellation" text and graphics from "Noise Cancellation," Ron Kurtus' School for Champions, http://www.school-for-champions.com/science/noise_cancellation.htm Copyright 2012 by Ron Kurtus. Reproduced with permission of Ron Kurtus.

"Prefrontal regulation during alert, non-stress conditions" graphic reprinted by permission from Springer Nature: Springer, *Nature Reviews Neuroscience,* Stress signalling pathways that impair prefrontal cortex structure and function, Amy Arnsten, 2009.

"Reward circuitry in the brain and sensation-seeking" graphic from National Institute on Drug Abuse; National Institutes of Health; U.S. Department of Health and Human Services. (2016, February). Understanding drug abuse and addiction: What science says. https://www.drugabuse.gov/publications/teaching-packets/understanding-drug-abuse-addiction/section-i/4-reward-pathway

"Sequence of puberty" chart and text excerpts from Payne, R. K. (2013). *Achievement for All: Keys to Educating Middle Grades Students in Poverty. Association for Middle Level Educators.* Reprinted with permission.

"Thinking about thinking" graphic from Crockett, H. (2017). *The Neuroscience of Dating.* Copyright 2017 by Heidi Crockett. Reprinted with permission.

"You are not allowed…" graphic by permission of Oxford University Press, from Choudhury, S., Blakemore, S.-J., & Charman, T. (2006). Social cognitive development during adolescence. *Social Cognitive and Affective Neuroscience, 1*(3), 165–174. http://doi.org/10.1093/scan/nsl024

EMOTIONAL
poverty

VOLUME 2

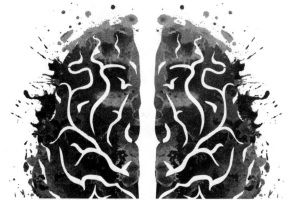

Safer Students and Less-Stressed Teachers

Ruby K. Payne, Ph.D.

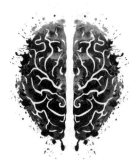

Table of Contents

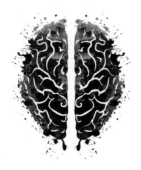

Dedication

This book is dedicated to the well-being of children and to all adults who work with them.

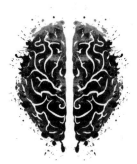

Acknowledgments

A very special thank you to Michael Curl and Norma Vijeila, both practicing principals. Thanks also to Peg Conrad, Jesse Conrad, and Paula Nicolella for their support in turning the book into a finished product. And an extra special thanks to my husband, Tee Bowman, for his patience and support.

Also, a very special thanks to the team of consultants who helped me develop the training and vet the ideas in the book. These individuals were Michael Curl, Norma Vijeila, Chestin Auzenne-Curl, Rickey Frierson, Bethanie Tucker, Jim Littlejohn, Kim Ellis, Marye Jane Brockinton, DeShanna King, Jen Nehl, and Kirven Tillis.

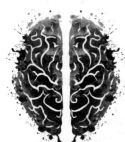 Introduction

Basic Review and Overview
of *Emotional Poverty*

This book is a follow-up to *Emotional Poverty in All Demographics.* That book examined the unregulated, unintegrated brain; calming techniques; what motivates good/healthy behaviors (compassion for self and others) and bad/ unhealthy behaviors (little compassion for self and others); why discipline works with some students and not others; why external environments that reinforce "less than" and "separate from" perceptions create more anger and violence; male brains and some of the issues with emotional processing; and the emotional noise in a classroom and how adults contribute to that noise.

The following are some basic concepts that were in *Emotional Poverty:*

1. All emotional wellness is based in safety and belonging.

2. It is difficult to change behavior. It is much easier to change the *motivation* for the behavior, which then changes the behavior.

3. The biggest difference between healthy (beneficial) and unhealthy (unbeneficial) behavior is compassion—for yourself and others.

4. Schools will always have consequences. It is the approach that needs to change.

5. The amygdala is mostly structured by the time you are three years old. It is restructured in adolescence.

6. At their base level, emotions are simple—you are either moving toward something or away from something. That is why it is not possible for the brain to be both angry and compassionate at the same time. Anger is an "away from" emotion that often results in attack. Compassion is a "moving toward" emotion that usually results in understanding.

7. To change a behavior or response, the behavior or response has to be named.

> **Please note:** This approach does not see a difficult student/person as "bad" or "sick" but rather as someone who is injured. *Emotional Poverty* looks at how to approach a person so that everyone—both individuals and organizations—can function at a higher level of safety and belonging.

This book will pick up and add to the discussion by looking at:

- How the limbic system "tells" emotions and stressors.
- How the energy system of the body can be reset to lessen stress and calm students.
- The development of adolescent brains.
- How to develop the prefrontal cortex and build emotional muscle (resilience) in students.
- How the hippocampus develops the stories of ourselves through coauthors and early childhood experiences that shape adult strengths and weaknesses.
- Tools for adults who are stressed and have compassion fatigue or secondary traumatic stress.
- How to work with angry, emotional parents and adults.

> **Disclaimer**
>
> This book looks at patterns and basic understandings. It does not explain every behavior/emotional reality. Not all of this information will apply to students in special education with a 504 or an IEP. The purpose of this book is to provide the language to name what educators are seeing and strategies to address some of those issues.

This book is for practitioners—not for psychologists. It is for individuals who work with children and adolescents and need a vocabulary and strategies for addressing emotional issues. Practitioners, unless they work in psychology or counseling, rarely get this information. My books on emotional poverty translate clinical research into understandings that can be used by practitioners. It is my hope that these books will give educators and other care providers the basic language for naming the emotional issues and provide strategies to address the behaviors.

> **The limits of my language mean the limits of my world.**
>
> –Ludwig Wittgenstein[1]

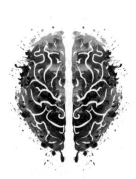

1 The Limbic Center

The emotional center of the brain—the amygdala

1. **How to watch body "tells" to determine emotional distress**
2. **How to use the energy systems of the body to reduce emotional distress**
3. **How to use these tools to keep your campus safer**

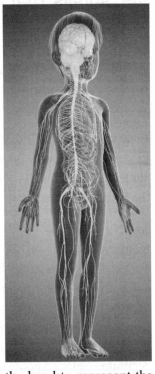

As discussed in my first book on emotional poverty, when you have an "in your face" explosion, the reality is that you are witnessing an unregulated and unintegrated brain. Before any kind of rational discussion can be had, it is important to allow time for the blood flow to return to the cortex of the brain where thoughts are. When the brain "explodes," the blood flow in the brain goes to the brain stem (the survival center of the brain) and leaves the cortex (where the thoughts are). It is not possible for the brain to understand a conversation until the blood flow returns to the cortex.

As you will remember from the hand model—using the hand to represent the brain—your palm is the brain stem (involuntary and motivational systems), your thumb is the amygdala, the area around it is the hippocampus (together the amygdala and hippocampus make up the limbic or emotional center of the brain), and the cortex is the top of the brain where thoughts are. The two middle fingers are the prefrontal cortex, which is the regulator of the brain.

Because your brain is connected to the rest of your body, the limbic system of your body most accurately reflects what you are feeling. The cortex (your thoughts) can represent what you think you should say or what is socially acceptable, but your body often "tells" what your true stressors and feelings are. Because the limbic system reacts to your feelings without the intervention of thought, it is the most accurate "tell."

Your limbic system has three choices: freeze, take flight, or fight. When something happens in your environment, you will respond in one of these three ways. The automatic first choice is freeze. The second is flight. And the last is fight.

Promoting a Safer Building—Being Able to Read the Signals That the Emotional Part of the Brain Is Emitting

Emotions are processed much faster than thought (200–5,000 times faster), and they are processed before thought is processed. The body's response is immediate because the brain—the limbic system—wants to keep the rest of your body from danger; it wants to keep you safe.

Educators can watch students' bodies to get early indicators of where the student is emotionally—often before the student is aware.

Joe Navarro was an FBI agent for many years, and in his book, *What Every Body Is Saying,* he identifies a discomfort-detecting and pacifying approach to understanding emotional responses. These responses come from the limbic system and are accurate "tells" about the level of comfort/discomfort the individual is experiencing. Navarro used this system to help law enforcement officials identify the truth in many cases. However, he is very careful to say that there is no one way to identify the truth and that no system is totally accurate.

"Whenever there is a limbic response—especially to a negative or threatening experience—it will be followed by pacifying behaviors (or adaptors)."[2]

Which part of your body is the most honest? Your feet. Yes, that's right. "When it comes to honesty, truthfulness decreases as we move from the feet to the head."[3]

Why are your feet the most honest? Because any of these three responses—freeze, flight, or fight—requires your feet. Feet are often the first tell that the body exhibits when there is discomfort or stress. When individuals freeze, they are working to avoid being seen while they take time to assess the danger.

Freeze (first response)	Flight (next response)	Fight (last response)
• Stop movement • Hold breath or breathe from the chest • Restrict motion • Try to be invisible • If abused, may avoid contact; arms will go dormant trying not to be seen	• Need to get away • Turn away from the person • Evade conversation • Close or rub the eyes • Cover face with hands • Lean away • Turn feet toward exit • Distance oneself	• Attack • Not look at you • Verbal assault • Sarcasm, denigration • Lean forward toward you • Torso will begin moving

When the amygdala and the rest of the limbic system get triggered, the body prepares to either freeze, run, or fight. When that happens, blood goes to the legs and arms and away from the skin so that the body can freeze, run, or fight. When the blood flow leaves the skin, the body surface feels cooler, hands get cold, and skin tone may change.

What Is a Pacifying Behavior?

A pacifying behavior is a behavior that is meant to soothe yourself. Look for the pattern of discomfort followed by a soothing behavior. Pacifying behaviors help signal what things trouble or distress a person.

A pattern that often occurs is that the individual will signal discomfort—e.g., leaning away, frowning, crossed or tense arms. This signaling of discomfort is often followed by a pacifying behavior. The brain requires the body to do something that will stimulate nerve endings, which releases calming endorphins in the brain so that the limbic system can be soothed.

Examples of Pacifying Behaviors

- Neck touching or stroking; touching the suprasternal notch (the indented area below the Adam's apple and the breastbone—sometimes referred to as the neck dimple); *the neck has a lot of nerve endings and, when stroked, lowers blood pressure and heart rate*
- Massaging/stroking the face, playing with hair
- Exhaling slowly with puffed cheeks
- Using the tongue inside the mouth to massage cheeks or lips
- If chewing gum, will chew faster
- Touching head, face, neck, shoulder, arm
- Men may stroke face or beard, adjust ties
- Women may touch necks, clothes, jewelry, hair
- Tapping a pencil or drumming fingers
- Playing with objects—pens, lipstick, etc.
- Excessive yawning
- Leg cleansing—moving your hands up and down your legs

Note: The information that follows is about patterns. These patterns must be considered in context, and it is important to note the changes a person makes in the course of a conversation. It is the changes that are important to watch, particularly if they differ from that person's nonverbal tendencies. *No one indicator* is the whole picture. You must observe the patterns and combinations.

What to Look for in Legs/Feet

When you first meet someone, watch what the person does with their feet and legs. If the feet and legs stay where they are, the person is comfortable. If they turn their feet away from you, they would like to leave. If the feet and legs move away from you, the person wants space. If the feet and legs move toward you, the person likes you. If they wrap their legs around chair legs, this is a "freeze" position that indicates discomfort.

It is normal for people to jiggle and move their feet. If the feet stop moving, it is an indication of possible discomfort. If the feet kick up, a stress point has been touched. "Gravity defying behaviors"—e.g., heel on the ground but the rest of the foot pointed up—usually indicate comfort. "Gravity defying behaviors of feet and legs are rarely seen in people suffering from clinical depression."[4]

When individuals cross their legs, this indicates general comfort with the situation. Why? Because when your legs are crossed, it is difficult to run or fight. Leg direction when crossed indicates that the person likes the individual toward whom the legs are pointing.

Using the Legs and Feet for Territorial Displays

When the feet splay out, this is often a territorial display. Splayed feet allow for more balance and create more space (territory). Splayed feet generally indicate that something is wrong and the person is ready to deal with it. A person can reduce confrontation by bringing the legs and feet back together because standing with the

feet together is perceived as submissive. Navarro cautions women in leadership positions not to have their feet together because it indicates submission.

> [Cultural anthropologist Edward T.] Hall found that the more advantages we have socioeconomically or hierarchically, the more territory we demand. He also found that people who tend to take up more space (territory) through their daily activities also tend to be more self-assured, more confident, and of course more likely to be of high status. This phenomenon has been demonstrated throughout human history and in most cultures.[5]

In Relationships

In social and romantic relationships, women will shoe play—e.g., shoes on the tips of her toes, partly off, rubbing a leg/foot with her shoe; this indicates comfort. "The feet contain a tremendous number of sensory receptors, the pathways of which terminate in an area of the brain that is close to the place in which sensations of the genitalia are registered."[6]

What to Look for in Torso, Chest, Shoulders

Your torso is where many of your key organs are located. When a person is in distress, the limbic system instructs the body to protect that area.

When you meet someone, what is their torso doing? Are they leaning toward you? Unless they are angry, leaning toward you indicates comfort and interest in the situation. If they are moving away from you, this indicates discomfort. Is their torso facing your torso? Then they are probably comfortable with the situation. But if they shield their torso with an object or their arms or hands, this indicates discomfort.

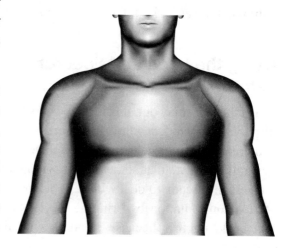

When the limbic system gets triggered and the body identifies the situation as a threat situation, the blood flow to the digestive system is reduced. The blood flow goes to the heart and legs in case there is a need to flee or fight. That is why people have difficulty eating and may even vomit when they are upset. The blood flow leaves the digestive system, and it is very difficult to eat.

What a person wears to cover their body is also important, as it sends a message. When people are mentally or physically ill, the posture of the torso and shoulders, as well as overall appearance, declines. "The phenomenon of poor grooming during illness and sadness has been documented around the world."[7]

Torso splaying (e.g., sprawling in a chair) when discussing a serious issue is disrespectful and shows indifference to those in authority. Puffing up the chest has been shown to be a strong indicator that a physical fight is about to begin. When the body is getting ready to fight, the chest will puff up, and the rate of breathing will increase. The body wants as much oxygen as possible.

What to Look for in the Arms

Arm movements indicate comfort or discomfort. When the movement is unrestrained—pointing, gesticulating, holding, lifting, hugging, waving—this generally indicates comfort and excitement. Elation and happiness are often expressed by holding the arms straight up in the air towards the sky.

Negative emotions bring us down. When we are injured, threatened, or worried, our arms come across our chests and/or come down. The phrase "to hold myself back" is often demonstrated by withdrawing the arms.

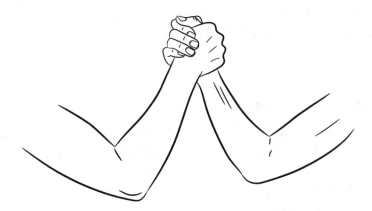

"Arm freeze" often occurs with children who have abusive parents or experience with predators. It is an attempt to freeze movement so that you are not noticed.

Arm-freeze behavior can serve to warn caring adults, whether teachers, neighbors, relatives, or friends, that a child might be the victim of abuse…[H]umans use their arms to defend themselves, a predictable limbic reaction. Because children use their arms to block their bodies as their primary means of defense (adults may use objects), a flailing arm is often the first thing an abusive parent will grab. Parents who aggressively seize children in this way will leave pressure marks on the ventral side (the inside) of the arms. Especially if the parent shakes the child in this position, the marks will be deeper in color (from greater pressure) and have the larger shape of the adult hand or the elongated shape of the thumb or fingers.[8]

Touch

One of the ways humans indicate that they do not want to be touched is to put their arms behind their backs. Arms behind the back can also carry the message "I am of higher status than you are." Humans dislike feeling that someone does not want to touch them, and so do animals.

Touching is very important. "Health, mood, mental development, and even longevity are said to be influenced by how much physical contact we have with others and how often positive touching takes place."[9]

The arms have large numbers of sensory receptors. Arm touching can be a source of pleasure. Arms touching someone usually indicates that we are comfortable with that person. People will move their arms away if they are uncomfortable with the person or something that person is saying. In Latin America, an *abrazo* (brief hug) says that I like you. An *abrazo* is when the chests meet and the arms engulf the back of the other person. It is very brief.

A brief touch on the arm means that our relationship is okay.

Other Arm Positions

Arms outspread can be another indicator of territorial display—e.g., taking up space and indicating dominance. Another indicator of dominance (or "I am in charge") is when the individual puts their hands behind their head and laces their fingers together.

Arms held akimbo indicate that you are standing your ground, confident, and will be difficult to bully. If arms akimbo are used in an aggressive situation—e.g., a potential fight—it often increases the aggression. Criminals identify the arms akimbo stance as one often adopted by law enforcement, and they use it to identify undercover officers.

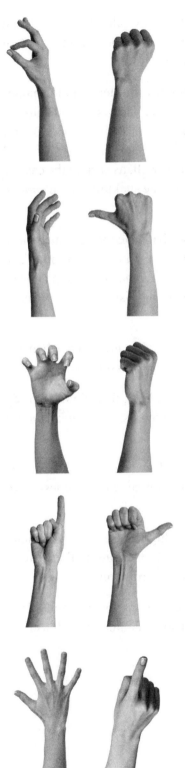

When a standing person is leaning on a table with the fingertips planted and the arms firmly apart, this is another power position that indicates confidence and authority. Gate attendants for airlines know that when a traveler positions their arms widely on the counter, there is a greater likelihood that there will be a confrontation.

To relax a stranger, stand with your arms relaxed, preferably with some of the inside of your arms showing, and if possible, with your palms up.

What Do the Hands and Fingers Tell You?

"Our brains give a disproportionate amount of attention to the wrists, palms, fingers, and hands as compared to the rest of the body."[10]

Hiding your hands creates a negative impression. Let people see them. Educators should not hide their hands behind a podium or desk. This is equated with dishonesty, holding back, possibly outright lying.

A handshake leaves an impression. Using the handshake as a way to establish power generally creates discomfort. The politician's handshake (covering the top of the handshake with the other hand) creates a negative effect for most people.

In any relationship, when there is more trust, there is more touching. If you ask a student if you can hold their hand during a conversation or while walking down the hall (especially in the early grades of elementary school), it establishes a level of communication and trust.

Finger pointing is viewed in a negative light worldwide.

Preening (self-care) should not be done when others are talking to you. It is a sign of dismissiveness. For example, think of trying to say something important to someone while they are clipping their fingernails.

When the limbic brain is stressed, surges of neurotransmitters and hormones (especially adrenaline) can cause the hands to shake. This is an indicator of stress. Sometimes when we are happy (e.g., when we have just won a prize), our hands will shake. The context becomes very important. Is this joy or fear? Neurological issues may cause the hands to shake as well, as seen in the case of Parkinson's disease, for example. Therefore it is not the shaking but the *change* that should be observed.

Individuals with more perceived status tend to use "hand steepling" much more because of their confidence. If confidence is shaken, the fingers may interlace (as they might in prayer). Women tend to steeple their hands under the table or low on the chest. Women need to make hand steepling visible if they want to convey confidence.

Hand-wringing indicates stress. Low confidence is also indicated when the thumbs are placed in the pockets and the fingers are left outside the pockets.

Genital framing on the part of men is when they will hook their thumbs inside their waistbands and let their fingers frame their genitals. Message: "I am a virile male. Look at me." It is a dominance display.

"Research tells us liars tend to gesture less, touch less, and move their arms and legs less than honest people."[11] In the face of a threat, we move less—we tend to freeze.

Interlacing of fingers is a very accurate indicator of high distress. It can include the rubbing of palms and fingers. Withdrawing hands and putting them under the table may indicate the individual is concealing information.

Micro-gestures of the hands—e.g., pushing the hands along the legs and lifting the middle finger at the final moment—indicate dislike, contempt, and disdain.

What Do the Face, Eyes, and Eyebrows Tell You?

Human beings can have more than 10,000 facial expressions. Facial expressions can be faked and are not as reliable as other parts of the body in terms of broadcasting genuine nonverbal communication. When the face is tense (tightened jaw, flared nostrils, quivering mouth, tightly compressed lips), it indicates negative emotions. Positive emotions show up in the following ways: loosening of the forehead lines, muscles around the mouth relax, lips are fuller, eye area is widened. Often, when people are truly relaxed, the head tilts, exposing our neck (and signaling openness or vulnerability).

Individuals will often use words that convey one thing while the nonverbals in the face convey the opposite.

Eyes

Eyes down indicates emotional processing, and if the shoulders are also slumped, it often indicates the processing of negative emotions. When we see something we like, our pupils dilate; when we see something we don't like, they constrict. Eye blocking is an indication that the individual has had a negative reaction to new information. Eye blocking can take the form of closing the eyes, covering the eyes with the hands, or rubbing a closed eye. Sometimes the eyes may be closed very tightly. Eye flashes indicate a pleasant surprise. When people look away during a conversation, they are thinking. They detect no threats from the other individuals. However, roving eyes leave a bad impression.

Eyebrows

People squint and their eyebrows lower when they are feeling aggressive, confrontational, annoyed, or angry. Eyebrows held too low are seen as signs of weakness and insecurity. In studies, "prisoners have reported that when new inmates arrive at jail, they look for this troubled, lowered-eyebrow behavior in the newcomers to reveal which ones are weak and insecure."[12]

Mouth

Everyone has a real smile and a fake smile. You can use a smile as a barometer of how someone really feels about you. A real smile forces the corners of the mouth up toward the eyes. In a fake smile, the corners of the mouth move toward the ears, and the eyes show little emotion.

A Story: Going to California

When I was a principal, I had a fifth-grade student sent to my office the week before Thanksgiving for getting into a fight at recess. I had never seen this student before. Generally, if you have not seen a student until Thanksgiving, the student is not a "frequent flyer" in terms of discipline referrals. When he came into my office, his body "tells" indicated a great deal of anxiety and stress. He was wringing his hands, his legs were restless, his feet were turned away from me, and he looked like he wanted to run.

In an attempt to calm him down, I asked him what he was going to do for Thanksgiving. He replied angrily, "Going to California. See my dad and his new wife."

I said, "I take it you do not want to go." He verified that.

I asked him if that was the reason he got into a fight, and he said yes.

So I said to him, "Well, you have another week of school. You cannot get in another fight. The first thing we need to do is make a plan for when you go to California. Have you met the new wife?" He said no. I asked if she had children, and he did not know that either. He knew almost nothing about the situation he was going to be in.

I asked him if he liked video games, books, and movies. The answer to all three was yes. (He was an affluent child.) So I said to him, "You need to take those with you so you have something to do because there are so many unknowns in this situation. Can you take those things with you?" He said he could.

Then I said, "We also have to make a plan so that you don't get in any more fights at school."

I taught him how to calm himself in this way: First, together we identified what his body did when he started thinking about the situation and got upset. I said, "When your body does those things, then you need to look at the ceiling, take several deep breaths through your nose with your lips closed to activate serotonin in the gut, and make your legs relax." Then I taught him how to close his eyes, visualize a safe place, and squeeze his wrists to remember that feeling of safeness.

I asked him, "When you go back to class, can you do these strategies?" He said yes. Then I said to him, "If you have a day when these strategies do not work for you, please tell the teacher that you need to come see me, and you can de-stress here in the office. But you cannot fight."

He did not get into any more fights.

I always had such empathy for this 11-year-old. The adults in his life obviously were so preoccupied with their own lives that they had given him few tools to deal with the situation.

How the Limbic System Is Tied into the Energy System of the Body and Cellular Memories

As the above story illustrates, the response of the limbic system is tied into the thoughts, emotions, and energy system of the body. One of the ways information gets carried throughout the body is via the vagus nerve. The vagus nerve is the longest nerve of the autonomic nervous system and connects to many parts of your body, including the spinal nerves and the major organs of your body.

The vagus nerve controls the autonomic nervous system, which has two parts—the sympathetic system (which is a fire alarm) and the parasympathetic system (which is a calming system). When a person gets stressed, the fire alarm goes off and sends a message down the vagus nerve to all parts of the body.

Part of the way the limbic system reacts is to cellular memories.

Memories Stored at the Cellular Level That You Do Not Know You Have

Memories are stored in the body at the cellular level in addition to being stored in the brain. In September 2004, *The Dallas Morning News* reported a study that was released by the University of Texas Southwestern Medical Center. "Throughout the natural world, scientists are finding, cells and organisms record their experiences, all without the benefit of a brain. Scientists believe these cellular memories might mean the difference between a healthy life and death."[13]

Increasingly, research is indicating that the human body records memories at the cellular level.

What happens in the body to prevent change is that cellular memories often operate out of fear and resist change. Fear is the mechanism that keeps you from being hurt again. If you have been abused, neglected, betrayed, etc., those memories are also stored at the cellular level.

"There are two other factors that arise with cellular memory. One is that memories are inherited from your ancestors just like your DNA."[14] The current research in epigenetics is indicating how true that is. If your parents or grandparents experienced trauma, it can change the way your genes are expressed.

The second factor is one in which you have destructive memories you don't know you have. Since so much of the emotional brain structuring is completed before you are three years old, memories get recorded as they are interpreted by a young child without language. Sometimes the way the memory is recorded is with a wrong interpretation. Alexander Loyd is a psychologist who tells the story of a client who, at the age of five, had an incident where her mother let her sister have a Popsicle but not her. The incident got recorded in her brain with the following interpretation: "If my mom gives my sister a Popsicle but doesn't give me one, it must mean that my mom loves my sister more than me. If my mom loves my sister more than me, then it must mean that something is wrong with me. If something is wrong with me, then when I get out here in the world, other people are not going to love me either, and I'm going to fail because there is something wrong with me."[15]

These cellular memories become a part of your body and impact your energy system. "Dr. Bruce Lipton talks about how any given cell in the body at any given moment is in one of two modes. It is either in growth mode or self-protection mode. Self-protection mode is the shut-down state of a cell that is in fight-or-flight mode."[16]

As people experience success, the pituitary gland releases oxytocin and vasopressin, which trigger the body's love and success mechanism.

How could something as seemingly insubstantial as a negative memory affect something as physical and measurable as hormones? Remember that everything is energy, including your cellular memories and your hormones. Both are vibrating at specific frequencies...Having too many negative memories would indicate that their combined frequencies overpower the effects of oxytocin and vasopressin.[17]

The Electromagnetic Energy System of the Body

Everything that happens in your body involves chemicals and electricity. These produce an electromagnetic field. This field goes out three feet from your body. That is one of the reasons why, when you are in a room with an angry person, you can feel their anger.

Electromagnetic Field of the Heart[18]

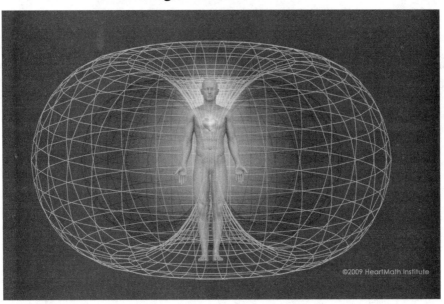

©2009 HeartMath Institute

The vibration of love is a huge factor in heart coherence and heart regulation.[19]

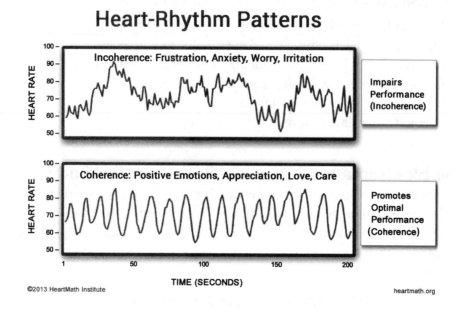

The HeartMath Institute provides this graph to show how the heartbeat between a boy and his dog are in sync when they get together.[20]

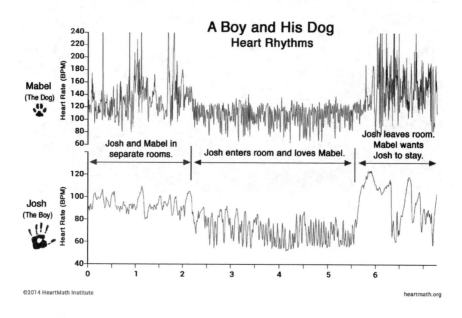

Energies and Vibrations Are Waves That Can Be Felt by Others

Energy is passed via electromagnetic waves from one human or animal to another, and this impacts your autonomic nervous system, which sends the message down your vagus nerve to the spine, organs, and body—including your solar plexus.

As you can see from the graphs, the energy that the teacher/educator brings into a situation impacts the energy of the student.

Biofield Research

"*Biofield therapies,* a term coined during the U.S. National Institutes of Health Conference, was first used in 1992…Biofields [are] endogenously generated fields, which may play a significant role in information transfer processes that contribute to an individual's state of mental, emotional, physical, and spiritual well-being."[21]

Our current Western medical practice uses a Newtonian physics approach to biology, chemistry, and the body by studying the physical parts, the chemicals in the body, and the systems in the body. In fact, the medical field is organized into specialties that focus on separate the parts of the body. For example, a neurologist, a urologist, an orthopedic surgeon, and a psychiatrist each focus on different parts of the body. To a large extent, current medical practice focuses on sickness and some preventive health. For most people, when they interface with the medical field, they are doing so out of sickness. In that model, the belief is that the individual will be healed by the medical profession, and the only way the individual participates is to take medication and do the prescribed exercises/rest.

The emerging field of functional medicine is based upon a quantum physics approach to biology and the body. In this model, the belief is that individuals can often heal themselves and that thoughts and emotions are often a part of medical issues. Functional medicine looks at the energy, chemical, mental, and emotional systems of the body, as well as the electromagnetic fields of the body. Caroline Myss is a medical intuitive who works with Harvard neurosurgeon Norm Shealy and is author of the book *Why People Don't Heal and How They Can.* She identifies the thoughts and emotions that may "create" the physical illness. Thoughts and emotions are energy patterns.

Fermilab in Batavia, Illinois, has known for years that the outcome of its atom-smashing experiment is different depending upon who is watching from the observation deck, even when the experiment is exactly the same. What they know is that the energies from human bodies impact the interactions of the atom splitting and create different outcomes.

What Strategies Can You Use to Further Calm Students?

1. Meditation

Sara Lazar, a neuroscientist at Massachusetts General Hospital and Harvard Medical School, decided to research meditation and its impact on the brain. "The study found differences in brain volume after eight weeks in five different regions in the brains of the two groups. In the group that learned meditation, the study identified thickening in four regions:

1. The primary difference was in the posterior cingulate, which is involved in mind wandering and self-relevance.

2. The left hippocampus, which assists in learning, cognition, memory, and emotional regulation.

3. The temporoparietal junction, or TPJ, which is associated with perspective-taking, empathy, and compassion.

4. An area of the brain stem called the pons, where a lot of regulatory neurotransmitters are produced."[22]

The fifth area of change was "the amygdala, the fight or flight part of the brain, which is important for anxiety, fear, and stress in general. That area got smaller in the group that went through the mindfulness-based stress reduction program. The change in the amygdala was also correlated to a reduction in stress levels."[23]

2. Mindfulness Training

What is the difference between meditation and mindfulness? The Chopra Center gives these examples: In meditation (there are different kinds: visualization, mantra, breath awareness, guided), for example in mantra meditation, one would breathe deeply and hum "om" repeatedly. If the inhaling is done with the lips closed, it activates the serotonin receptors in the abdomen and calms one down.[24]

Mindfulness training is when you simply focus on the present and do not let your mind wander. For example, looking at a flower and thinking only about the flower. It is a way to focus and regulate the brain.

Mindfulness training is being used in many schools to help students calm themselves. Recently I talked to a fifth-grade teacher in a high-poverty school who uses a singing bell to calm her students down after lunch, as well as other mindfulness tools. She has no discipline referrals.

I met an elementary principal from a high-poverty school in Illinois who uses mindfulness throughout her campus. She said that her discipline referrals have been cut in half.

3. Applied Kinesiology

Getting answers about "what's best for you" from your body. Your body knows your emotional truth.

Applied kinesiology (AK) is the emotional information that is transferred from the limbic system of the brain to the muscles. It can help determine what our bodies know is actually good or helpful for us.

AK was developed by Dr. George Goodheart, an American chiropractor, in the early 1960s. AK is also known as muscle testing, which is a type of bio-resonance testing. All matter (including the matter that makes up our bodies) is both particle and wave. In other words, it is both matter and energy. All energy has a frequency.

A strong response (e.g., the arm is firm) indicates that the person has a positive or neutral response.

A weak response (e.g., the arm drops) indicates that the person has a negative response.

Human bodies' electromagnetic energy field has a positive and negative polarity—i.e., a positive and negative response. Anything perceived to be harmful—a word, action, thought, food, emotion—will be identified by the energy in the body, even when the cortex (conscious mind) may not know it.

Muscle testing is when you ask a true/false question to the person and ask for a muscle response. The issue with muscle testing is that it can be inaccurate if the body is dehydrated or if the person is tired.

Make a true/false statement and then press the arm. If the arm stays strong, basically that choice is good for you. If your arm drops, that choice is less good for you.

Basics of Muscle Testing

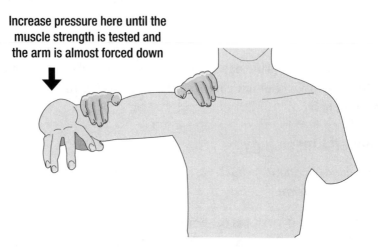

Increase pressure here until the muscle strength is tested and the arm is almost forced down

A consultant of mine, Ruben, is a behavioral specialist. He had a middle school student who was absolutely convinced that it was in his (the student's) best interest to drop out of school and be jumped into a gang. After a rather long conversation, Ruben was unable to convince the student not to go through with it. He said to the student, "Let me ask you two questions." He asked the student to hold out his arm. Then he asked the student, "Is it okay if I push on your arm?" The student said yes.

Then he said to the student, "It is in your best interest to get jumped into the gang." Ruben pushed the boy's arm, and his arm dropped. Then Ruben said to the boy, "It is in your best interest to do your homework, get better grades, and finish school." Ruben pushed on the boy's arm, and it held steady and did not drop. Ruben explained to the student what he was doing, and the student was stunned. He did not know what to say. The student stayed in school.

Some people find that their nondominant arm/hand is more responsive. Either arm will work. Before you test, make the statement. Touch the arm with the same force after each statement.

Alexander Loyd has other methods that are sometimes more accurate and do not involve touching the student or the person. They are based on the same concept of muscle testing but are more resistive to muscle fatigue.[25]

Here are two other methods:

Thumbs up—Hold your arm straight. Make a fist with your hand, but keep your thumb straight up. Make a statement. Now rotate your hand until the hand stops moving. Where is your thumb pointing? Note where it stops. Return your thumb to the straight-up position. Now say the opposite of the statement you said before. Rotate your hand. Where does your thumb stop? Your thumb will rotate farther for a true statement.

Double pistol—Put your hands together, fingers interlaced as if you were praying. Make a gun with your index fingers together pointing. Your arms will be straight out. Your thumbs will be pointing up. Make a statement and watch how high the tips of your index fingers go up. Make the opposite statement and watch how high the tips of your index fingers go up. Your index fingers will rise higher after a true statement.

For more of these techniques, read *The Truth Techniques* by Alexander Loyd.

Here are interventions that help regulate and balance the autonomic nervous system of your body, which the vagus nerve controls. These are taken from the book *101 Trauma-Informed Interventions* by Linda Curran. These also reduce stress.

1. Yawning

HOW? Feel the joints of your jaw. Massage those muscles. Open your mouth—then open it wider—and open your throat. Inhale from your gut. At the end of the inhalation, exhale loudly with a sigh or huff. Allow your breathing to return to normal.

WHY? Yawning is a respiratory reflex that improves circulation to the face, relaxes the eyes, and forces you to breathe from your gut as opposed to breathing from your chest. Yawning helps your body relax. Your jaws tend to be the tensest muscles in your body.

2. Cross Crawl

HOW? March in place, raising each leg in turn with the opposing arm. Try to do the exercise slowly, and take a few hundred steps in place, being careful not to fatigue your muscles.

WHY? The exercise regenerates connections in your nerves across your body in the same way that happens when an infant learns to crawl or when an athlete practices a particular motion.

3. Hand Warming

HOW? Just rub your hands together, or use disposable hand warmers or warm water. When a person gets upset, the blood flow leaves their hands. Warming them has a calming effect.[26]

WHY? Stress sends blood away from our hands and feet so it can go to the vital organs and muscles. The more stressed a person is, the lower the temperature of their hands. "Research has shown that stress causes at least a one- to two-degree Fahrenheit decrease over a five minute period."[27]

Chapter Summary

1. The emotional "tells" from the limbic system allow you to have a safer campus. You are better able to read the emotional status of the students and know when they are stressed.

2. The muscle-testing/truth techniques allow you to help students understand what is in their best interest and where they are emotionally.

3. For those students who are on your emotional triage list, these techniques allow you to monitor much more accurately what their emotional state is. For more on triaging students according to emotional need, see my first book on emotional poverty.

4. Understand that memories held at the cellular level also trigger responses.

5. Electromagnetic waves impact behavior and relationships.

Developing the Prefrontal Cortex

Building regulation and emotional stability

The Prefrontal Cortex

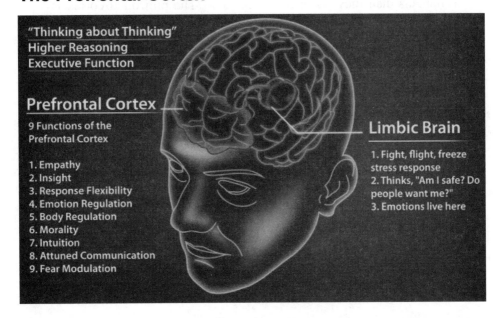

"Thinking about Thinking"
Higher Reasoning
Executive Function

Prefrontal Cortex

9 Functions of the
Prefrontal Cortex

1. Empathy
2. Insight
3. Response Flexibility
4. Emotion Regulation
5. Body Regulation
6. Morality
7. Intuition
8. Attuned Communication
9. Fear Modulation

Limbic Brain

1. Fight, flight, freeze
stress response
2. Thinks, "Am I safe? Do
people want me?"
3. Emotions live here

The graphic above is from *The Neuroscience of Dating* by Heidi Crockett. Crockett states: "In this chart, 'prefrontal cortex' and its nine functions technically refer to what's called the 'middle prefrontal cortex' in interpersonal neurobiology. This region comprises the medial and ventral prefrontal, orbitofrontal, and anterior cingulate cortices."[28]

What Does the Prefrontal Cortex Do?

The prefrontal cortex regulates the brain and does planning, impulse control, executive function, and working memory. It is where you hold information while you begin to process it. Interestingly, in adolescents, the brain develops from the back to the front. The front of the brain—the prefrontal cortex—develops last.

Much of the brain information we have is collected with MRI scans. "MRI (magnetic resonance imaging) combines radio waves, strong magnetic fields, and sophisticated computer technology to provide detailed information about the anatomy and physiology of the brain."[29]

The prefrontal cortex is bigger in humans relative to body size than in almost any other species. The cells in this area also look different in humans than they do in other animals. "The prefrontal cortex is where decisions are made, where temptations are muted, and where self-evaluation arises," writes Sarah-Jayne Blakemore.[30]

The following chart is based on information from the article "Neuropsychology of Prefrontal Cortex" by Shazia Veqar Siddiqui et al.

Aspects	Tasks
Executive functions	<ul><li>Initiate and execute new and goal-directed behaviors</li><li>Sustain attention to events in motor or action sequence</li><li>Short-term memory</li><li>Control interference and filter for information processing</li><li>Working memory</li><li>Planning, flexibility, delayed response, active problem solving</li><li>Emotional regulation</li><li>Detection of important aspects and sequencing of those aspects</li></ul>
Memory	<ul><li>Encoding and retrieval of memory</li><li>Recent memory</li><li>Source memory (contextual factors)</li><li>Sequential memory</li><li>Sequencing of temporal memory (time)</li></ul>
Intelligence	<ul><li>Verbal expression and memory</li><li>Abstraction</li><li>Ability to formulate plans and pursue them to goals</li><li>Spatial relationships between self and environment (self-reflective)</li><li>Use visual, spatial, and other information to inform and guide tasks</li></ul>
Language	<ul><li>Spontaneous speech</li><li>Narrative expression (stories or sequences)</li><li>Verbal fluency</li></ul>
Visual search and gaze control	<ul><li>Analyze details in pictures</li><li>Attend to all pertinent details in a scan</li></ul>

The Prefrontal Cortex Is the Regulator for Behavior

Daniel Amen is a psychiatrist who uses brain scans to identify physical, chemical, structural, and processing issues in brains.[31]

This is a picture of a healthy brain. There is full, even, symmetrical activity when the brain is healthy. The back of the brain is the cerebellum and has the activity shown in this picture.

Images I.1 and I.2: Healthy SPECT Scans

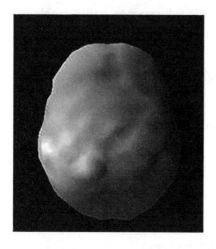 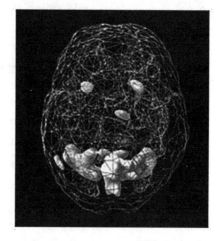

SURFACE
Full, even, symmetrical activity

ACTIVE
White equals the most active part of the brain, typically in the cerebellum in the back, bottom area

A damaged brain looks different. Here is one scan in which the brain has been damaged by drug abuse. There are holes in the cortex, the part of the brain where thoughts are processed. Compare this with the scan of a brain that has been damaged through an injury.

Image I.6: Drug Abuse

Damage seen across the cortex of the brain

Image I.5: Traumatic Brain Injury

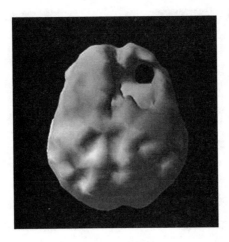

Damage to the right front side

ADHD (attention deficit hyperactivity disorder, previously known as ADD) is a brain issue in the prefrontal cortex. This is what the brain looks like when there is low frontal lobe activity.

Image I.12: ADD

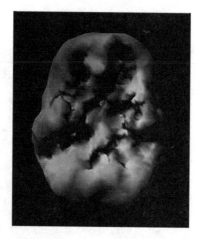

UNDERSIDE SURFACE
Low frontal lobe activity

In this picture of the ADHD brain, you will note the stress the student is under when he tries to concentrate. There is a marked decrease in the prefrontal cortex activity.

Images 10.1 and 10.2: Kent's ADD-Affected Brain, at Rest and Concentration

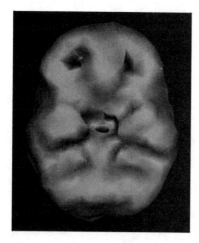

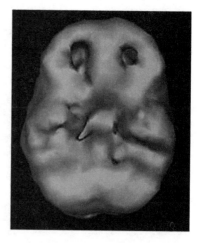

At rest; note overall good activity

During concentration; note markedly decreased PFC activity

When the prefrontal cortex is not developed or not functioning at an optimal level, Amen identifies these patterns. Here is a quiz from his book, *Change Your Brain, Change Your Life.*[32]

0 = never
1 = rarely
2 = occasionally
3 = frequently
4 = very frequently

1. Inability to give close attention to detail
2. Trouble sustaining attention in routine situations (homework, chores, paperwork, etc.)
3. Trouble listening
4. Inability to finish things, poor follow-through
5. Poor organization of time or space
6. Distractibility
7. Poor planning skills
8. Difficulty expressing feelings and emotions
9. Difficulty expressing empathy for others
10. Excessive daydreaming
11. Boredom
12. Conflict seeking
13. Difficulty awaiting turn
14. Impulsivity (saying or doing things without thinking first)
15. Frequent traffic violations

Amen states the following:

> In evaluating more than six thousand children with ADD [ADHD], Dr. Lubar found that the basic problem with these children is that they lack the ability to maintain 'beta' concentration states for sustained periods of time. He also found that these children have excessive 'theta' daydreaming brain-wave activity. Dr. Lubar found that through the use of EEG biofeedback, children could be taught to increase the amount of 'beta' brain waves and decrease the amount of 'theta,' or daydreaming brain waves.[33]

Brain Wave Patterns[34]

Pattern	Wave cycles per second	Description
Delta	1 to 4	Very slow—usually sleeping
Theta	5 to 7	Slow—daydreaming, twilight zone
Alpha	8 to 12	Relaxed
SMR (sensorimotor)	12 to 15	Focused relaxation
Beta	13 to 24	Fast—concentration or work

In other words, when a student is daydreaming, sleeping, or relaxed, the brain waves are different and elicit a different response from the student. To concentrate, the student needs to be functioning at the beta wave level: 13–24 wave cycles per second. When a student is not concentrating, the student is unable to maintain beta waves.

When the Prefrontal Cortex Gets Stressed

When the prefrontal cortex gets stressed, it is hijacked by the amygdala. The emotional self takes over—or as Steven Stosny says, the "toddler brain" is in control.

The following illustrations were published in the *National Review of Neuroscience* by Amy Arnsten.[35]

As you can see in the illustration, when the student is alert and not in stress (which would be a brain wave of 12 cycles per second or greater), the prefrontal cortex is in charge. The brain is able to do the following: reality testing, error monitoring, cortex (top-down) guidance for thoughts and attention, inhibit inappropriate actions, and regulate emotions.

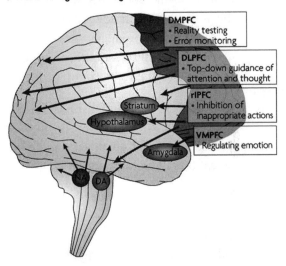

a Prefrontal regulation during alert, non-stress conditions

But, when the individual gets stressed, the amygdala hijacks the prefrontal cortex.

Survival (bottom-up guidance), emotional habits, emotional reflexes (habituated neural pathways), and emotional associations (triggers) take over. Emotional associations and reflexes include those that are stored at the cellular level and at the subconscious level in the "toddler brain." Often the individual has no language or understanding of the response.

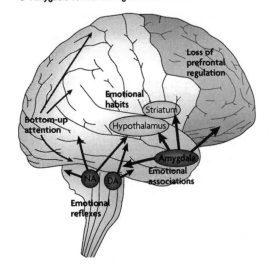

b Amygdala control during stress conditions

Anxiety: Does It Come from Your Amygdala or Cortex?

The answer is both. Sometimes it is from the amygdala and sometimes the cortex. In their book *Rewire Your Anxious Brain,* the authors explain how anxiety has two different sources: "The cortex pathway produces worries, obsessions, and interpretations that create anxiety...and the amygdala initiates bodily reactions that make up the fight, flight, or freeze response."[36]

Basically, as neurobiologist Carla Shatz has said, neurons that fire together wire together. In other words, the more times you think a thought or do an action, the more likely it is that you will repeat that thought or action.

The body responds to stress through the amygdala. Processing in the amygdala occurs in milliseconds. In addition, the amygdala decides whether the threat is dangerous or not. The following are indicators of a stress (amygdala) response: increased heartbeat, breathing rapidly from the upper chest area (not the abdomen), stomach pain, diarrhea, wanting to run or freeze, perspiring, and trembling. When these things happen, the amygdala has hijacked the cortex.

All of these are indicators of panic attacks. In a panic attack, the amygdala is responding to a trigger that often the person does not know they have. Panic attacks often lead to agoraphobia, which is a fear of being in a situation in which the person has had panic attacks before. Panic attacks are incredibly unpleasant and can become dangerous if left untreated. I have a friend who has panic attacks. He is a big man. He is terrified of having one because he knows that he can hurt someone else when he has one. If you or someone you know is experiencing panic attacks, be sure to seek help from a medical professional.

Tools for Dealing with Panic Attacks

1. Deep breathing from the abdomen. The way to do this is to breathe through the nose with the lips shut. Exhale with the lips open. The abdomen has many serotonin receptors (calming), and when the lips are closed, you are forced to breathe through your abdomen.

2. Eyes up on the ceiling. It is not possible for the brain to access feelings when the eyes are on the ceiling.

3. Distractions—think of something else.

4. Ice in the mouth and on the stomach.

5. Rewire your amygdala. There is a technique called active coping strategy that switches the freeze response to movement. What the person does is become very active: walking, running, moving, talking on the phone, or being involved with a game on a device.[37]

When the Anxiety Comes from the Cortex

When the anxiety comes from the cortex, it initially comes through your senses. When information comes into your brain through your senses, it goes through the thalamus, which is like a central relay station. The thalamus then sends the information to the lobes. The frontal lobes (the prefrontal cortex covers the frontal lobes) allow one to anticipate and interpret. It allows us to plan and to worry. When people worry, they anticipate negative outcomes. Their minds engage in "what if" thinking rather than "what is." It should be noted that the information from the thalamus can bypass the cortex and go straight to the amygdala. The amygdala has a longer memory system than the cortex. In fact, the amygdala memory system and the cortex memory system are different.[38] This means you can have a reaction to a situation and not know why.

Obsessive-compulsive disorder is when the frontal cortex engages in negative thoughts that will not go away. There is some evidence that obsessive thoughts are related to an issue in the cingulate cortex, an area just behind the eyes.[39]

"Children who have a smaller left amygdala tend to have more anxiety difficulties than other children."[40]

Part of dealing with anxiety is to assign language to the experience. As long as the anxiety is considered instinctual and not named, it will be difficult to address.

Symptoms of anxiety disorders are evident in what causes you to panic, what you avoid, and what makes you worry.

Situations/locations/ comments that make me uneasy/anxious	Where does my body react?	How do I feel? (afraid, angry, sad...)

What Are My Triggers?

What is it (action, comment, situation) that will trigger a negative response from me every time?

Addressing Triggers

"The language of the amygdala is based on associations...Triggers are associated with negative events."[41]

In the book *Rewire Your Anxious Brain,* the authors give an example of a woman who was raped. What brought on a panic attack for this woman was the smell of the cologne that the man who raped her was wearing. The association the amygdala made was with the cologne. Triggers can be something that was seen, a smell, a particular sound, or a unique situation.

There can be a combination of triggers. For example, I once hydroplaned across three lanes of a highway. Thankfully no one was hurt. But to this day, if it starts raining really hard and it becomes very difficult to see, I will pull off the road until the storm has passed. My heart rate will go up, and I will start breathing from my upper chest. I know what is happening. To ease my anxiety, I will simply pull off the road.

The trigger comes before the negative event. For example, in my case, it started raining hard before I hydroplaned. My amygdala was wired to recognize that if this happens (the trigger), then the negative event will follow.

You don't react to the negative event; rather, you react to the trigger.

Between the trigger and the emotional event is an interpretation (prefrontal cortex).

In my hydroplaning example:

Trigger	Interpretation	Negative response/ fear	Coping strategy
Heavy rain	I am going to be in an accident and possibly die	Elevated heart rate, rapid breathing	Pull off the road and wait for the storm to pass

Devastating kinds of triggers:

- Triggers that keep you from achieving your life goals
- Triggers that occur frequently
- Triggers that cause extreme distress

When individuals let anxiety take over, there is almost always erroneous thinking.

These are some kinds of erroneous thinking that individuals engage in:

1. All or nothing
2. Mind reading
3. Labeling
4. Blaming
5. What if rather than what is
6. Always
7. Identifying the negative
8. Predicting the future
9. Using only your feelings
10. Internal voice of guilt
11. Going from possibility to probability in a nanosecond

You can use the following chart with students.

Anxiety Creators

Comment	Kind of thinking	If...then...
No one likes me.	All or nothing	If my mom likes me, other people can like me also.
I am no good at math.	Identifying the negative	If I can keep track of my cellular data usage, I can do math.
She made me do it.	Blaming	If I give her that much power, I can also give myself that much power.
The principal called my mother. I am in trouble.	Possibility to probability	If the principal called my mom, then I need to find out what happened.
I hate her.	Using only feelings	If I can feel hate, then I can also find things to love.

How Does the Prefrontal Cortex Impact Learning?

Human Learning Process[42]

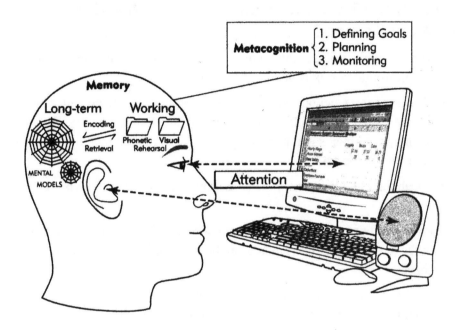

- You have to manage the irrelevant working memory load. Working memory is like the neck of a bottle in that it limits what can get into the brain—usually about 4–5 pieces of new information at one time. When working memory gets overloaded, it shuts off any new information within 12 seconds. Stress (allostatic load) will further reduce the amount down to one or two pieces of information at a time.

- Working memory takes in information in two main channels: auditory and visual. When we ask students who are new to the information we are providing to use a third channel, the information dropouts start. For example, if the teacher is lecturing (auditory) and using a slide presentation (visual) and asks the student to take notes (kinesthetic), the student for whom this is new learning will not be able to absorb it all and will start losing information. It is much better to have the students listen to the lecture and see the presentation. After the presentation, give them the notes, and have them work with a partner to highlight the notes.

What Does This Information Mean in the School or Work Setting?

- You have to teach students to plan (build executive function) because the prefrontal cortex is not as developed.

- Visual images (mental models) can be used to translate new ideas to the concrete. Visual imaging capability is not affected by poverty. Because the hippocampus is not as developed for learning and memory, visuals help students learn.

- Vocabulary acquisition can be taught by using sketching, a visual activity.

- Procedural processes must be taught. These build executive function in the prefrontal cortex. Details can be managed using visuals and step sheets.

- Well-organized, non-chaotic schools and classrooms reduce allostatic load. Classroom management is a must because it allows working memory to function better.

- Link reward systems to planning by giving rewards to recognize completion of a plan. This helps develop the prefrontal cortex.

- Use visuals to translate from the concrete sensory world to the abstract representational world of paper, ideas, numbers, letters, drawings, etc.

- Question making helps students deal with nonroutine tasks and problem solving (builds executive function).

- There will be more behavioral issues in poverty because of the larger amygdala and smaller hippocampus. Regulation of behavior must be taught.

- The role of nurturance—relationships—in the modulation of allostatic load and gene expression is important in learning.

What Are Strategies to Develop the Prefrontal Cortex?

Function	Strategy
Empathy	• Volunteering • Helping another student
Insight	• Study of literature and history when the approach is "why" (can be done through video)
Response flexibility	• If you choose…then you have chosen… • Muscle testing: Was that your best choice? • What are the choices of response you have in this situation? Which of these could you have done instead?
Emotional regulation	• Practice and rewire the response
Body regulation	• Eyes up, ice chips
Morality	• Character education, focusing on integrity, thoughtfulness, empathy
Intuition	• Learn how to sense what your body is telling you
Attuned communication	• Mirror neurons and mirroring behavior • Language choices
Fear modulation	• Is related to "What if"; Byron Katie's four questions

How Do You Get Emotional Stability?

Emotional stability is when you have the emotional strength and stamina to deal with an emotional hit. What is an emotional hit? Anything that jeopardizes safety and belonging. Safety and belonging are the foundation of emotional wellness.

You can rewire your brain. It takes 7–21 days to establish a new pattern.

How do you know when you have emotional stability? Emotionally stable people exhibit these characteristics:

1. They are reliable. If they say they are going to do something, they do it.
2. They are realistic. They rarely use the word "should." As author Byron Katie says, "should" is an argument with reality.
3. They can articulate how they are feeling with words and without blame.
4. Comments about them are not taken personally.
5. They operate out of mutual respect. They give mutual respect and accept it.
6. They do not tell you how to think or feel in a given situation. They may say how they think and feel but do not force their opinions on you.
7. They have boundaries and honor yours.
8. They are consistently fair and courteous.
9. They give back.
10. They are flexible and even-tempered.
11. They are kind with their feedback and comments.
12. They are patient and rarely irritated.
13. They understand that neural pathway development is related to habit formation.

Role of Integrity and Emotional Stability

One of the correlates to emotional stability is integrity. In the research on counterproductive behavior in the workplace, there is more emotional stability in an individual when integrity is in place.

How do you develop integrity in students? This has long been avoided in schools because it is seen as either values training, religious influence, or a conservative attempt at oppression. However, codes of behavior have been a part of every society. Alexis de Tocqueville, who wrote *Democracy in America,* is still considered one of the best writers on democracy. In *Democracy in America,* he indicates that the reason democracy works is that there is a set of commonly shared values that allows the society to function without a heavy police presence.

I was in Charlotte, North Carolina, at Sugar Creek Charter School. It is more than 90% poverty, serving mostly minoritized students, and operates on a lottery system. They have a "character and career development program" starting in kindergarten. I watched kindergarten students talking about purpose, how to treat others well, consideration, and kindness.

Put in a character program at your school or in your district. It will make a huge difference in emotional stability. The Association of American Educators recommends character education programs on its website. They include Character First! Education, I CAN Character Curriculum, and Lessons in Character.[43]

Require that a part of the character program is volunteering. In the research, "the mental and emotional benefits of volunteering are even greater, with 93% reporting an improved mood, 79% reporting lower stress levels, and 88% reporting increased self-esteem by giving back. Also, volunteers are significantly more likely to feel they have greater control over their health and well-being."[44]

Chapter Summary

1. Brain damage and environments impact the prefrontal cortex. ADD and ADHD are physical issues as well as chemical issues.

2. Instructional tools can help develop the prefrontal cortex and assist learning.

3. Anxiety can come from both the prefrontal cortex and the amygdala.

4. The "if...then..." strategy can help reduce anxiety that comes from the prefrontal cortex.

5. Identifying triggers can reduce anxiety coming from the amygdala.

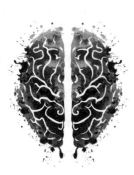

Adolescent Brain Development

Puberty, reward circuitry, risk-taking, and social cognition

The Theater of Adolescence

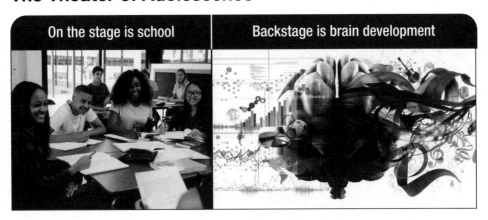

On the stage is school | Backstage is brain development

What is driving the brain development? Puberty (sex hormones) and sexual identity, social dominance, risk/reward circuitry, social cognition, and perspective-taking.

Is it any wonder that secondary schools are theaters of seething, churning emotional realities?

There are two different agendas occurring daily. One is the agenda of school. The other is the agenda of brain development. Schools ignore the incredible demands of brain development during adolescence.

This chapter will look at aspects of brain development that impact interactions with adolescent students (middle through high school).

In particular, these aspects are important:

1. Puberty, hormones, sexual identity, and gender development and their impact on the brain and socialization, including social dominance and bullying.

2. Reward center of the brain and how drugs, pornography, and screen time can change the brain.

3. Sensation-seeking and risk-taking parts of the brain and their development.

4. The development of perspective-taking during adolescence, including its influence on moral development.

5. The development of social cognition and its critical role in adolescent development.

6. Suggestions for schools to provide more emotional stability for adolescents.

Joshua

Written by Norma Vijeila, principal of an alternative school in California

Being an educator for many years, I have come to realize that there are many factors that can affect students' behavior. One factor in particular opened my eyes to the sudden change we saw in one of our young male students.

Joshua was a 16-year-old young man. His caretaker from a young age had been his paternal grandmother. He was respectful and responsible. He had never been in any kind of major trouble until recently.

One Monday morning his grandmother came to the school to notify us that Joshua had been arrested over the weekend. It was a shock to hear that he had been arrested for participating in an armed robbery using a BB gun that looked very realistic. Grandma came to talk to some of his teachers and the administrators to notify us of his arrest. She also wanted his teachers to write a character letter that could potentially be used to demonstrate that he had never been in any kind of trouble.

For a few weeks before his arrest, we had seen Joshua's attitude and behavior completely change. The first incident occurred when he disrespected a male teacher. The second incident was reported by a female teacher who reported that Joshua was being defiant to get the attention of other students, particularly females. The third incident occurred when he was found smoking marijuana in front of the school. His grandmother had shared that Joshua was now befriending a small group of older males.

Joshua was released from juvenile hall just a few days after being detained. He was placed on house arrest and was to wear an ankle monitor. When he returned to school, it was obvious that something had changed in this young boy. His attire, posture, attitude, acquaintances, and his interest in school were different. He had transformed in a matter of a few weeks, and we could not figure out what was happening to him.

One day, one of his teachers came into my office to talk to me about Joshua. She was reaching out for support to get him on the best track since his behavior had not improved. I asked the teacher to tell me what she thought was the event that took place to cause such changes. The female teacher looked at me and said, "I hope I don't get in trouble…but I think he had sex for the first time." I thought it was very brave of his teacher to say this because we don't typically discuss how sex may impact teens' identity and behavior. Although sexual encounters may not affect young people in the same way, sexual activity may have affected this young man's emotional self.

Before we discuss brain changes during adolescence, it is important to understand puberty and its impact on the brain. Puberty brings with it the pruning of the brain.

> The biggest issue for adolescents ages 10–15 is *puberty.* And the biggest issue about puberty that concerns adolescents is simply: *Am I going through the physical changes at about the same time as my friends?* Too early or too late, and they lose status with their peers. There can be up to three years of variation either way in all the changes adolescents go through during puberty, depending on the genetics and ethnicity of an adolescent. The average girl is two years ahead of the average boy in height changes. A girl's height spurt generally occurs before *menarche*—the first menstrual period—but the boy's height spurt usually takes place after *spermarche*—his first ejaculation. Kathleen Berger summarizes many of the physical changes middle grades students go through in the following chart.[45]

Sequence of Puberty

Girls	Approximate Average Age*	Boys
Ovaries increase production of estrogen and progesterone[1]	9	
Uterus and vagina begin to grow larger	9½	Testes increase production of testosterone[1]
Breast "bud" stage	10	Testes and scrotum grow larger
Pubic hair begins to appear; weight spurt begins	11	
Peak height spurt	11½	Pubic hair begins to appear
Peak muscle and organ growth (also, hips become noticeably wider)	12	Penis growth begins
Menarche (first menstrual period)	12½	Spermarche (first ejaculation); weight spurt begins
First ovulation	13	Peak height spurt
Voice lowers	14	Peak muscle and organ growth (also, shoulders become noticeably broader)
Final pubic hair pattern	15	Voice lowers; visible facial hair
Full breast growth	16	
	18	Final pubic hair pattern

*Average ages are rough approximates, with many perfectly normal, healthy adolescents as much as three years ahead of or behind these ages.
[1]Estrogens and testosterone influence sexual characteristics, including reproduction. Charted here are the increases produced by the gonads (sex glands). The ovaries produce estrogens, and the testes produce androgens, especially testosterone. Adrenal glands produce some of both kinds of hormones (not shown).

Research shows the major importance to teens of their peers' acceptance of the physical changes they are undergoing. It also shows that early onset of puberty is a huge risk factor for them and that later onset of puberty also carries risks. The chart on the following page is a compilation of information from Berger about some of the risk factors of early and late maturing of girls and boys.[46]

Risk Factors in Early and Late Maturing of Girls and Boys

	Early Maturing	Late Maturing
Girls	• Lower self-esteem • More depression • Earlier sexual activity • Higher level of pregnancy • Harsh parenting • Correlates to absence of biological father • Lower grades and the likelihood of course failure in ninth grade • More vulnerable to sexual abuse	• Four times the rate of self-harm (cutting, poisoning, etc.) • Poorer body image
Boys	• More aggressive • More delinquency • More alcohol abuse • More early sex • Correlates to absence of biological father • Lower grades and the likelihood of course failure in ninth grade	• More anxious, depressed, and afraid of sex • Four times the rate of self-harm (cutting, poisoning, etc.)

Note that if a young adolescent's parents are under the stress of illness, divorce, or addiction, or if they live in a violent environment, that young person is more likely to have earlier-onset puberty. Early puberty correlates with earlier sexual activity and with the absence of the biological father. Scientists do not agree on whether stress causes the early puberty or whether it's caused genetically.[47]

The Role of Social Dominance as a Part of Sexual Development

Despite the current rhetoric that there is no difference between males and females, there is significant research that would beg to differ. Nowhere is that debate more prevalent right now than in transgender issues and sports. The debate is currently "is it nature or nurture?" The review of the research would indicate that it is both/and rather than either/or.

Jordan Peterson, a clinical psychologist from Canada, in his book *12 Rules for Life,* goes back into the evolutionary patterns of animals and people. Most behaviors come from the need for status and position. Why? Because when resources are scarce, resources always go to those who have the most status, highest position, and most territory. Those three things allow one to have the greatest level of safety, belonging, and protection—and, therefore, *survival.* Peterson gives the examples of songbirds and lobsters. In fact, in the research on chickens, there is a "pecking order" among chickens. And as Peterson states, "territory-seeking produces conflict." Who is going to win the conflict? Who has dominance?

Lobsters have been around for 350 million years. In a research study, the researchers captured several male lobsters and relocated them to watch their behaviors. The researchers watched to see how they would establish order. Lobsters begin by exploring and finding good places to hide for protection. Because the best places to hide are scarce, this inevitably leads to conflict. In the lobster nervous system, there is a built-in set of defensive and aggressive behaviors.

The first approach is for a lobster to dance around, evade, and open and shut its claws. Each lobster has the ability to spray liquid at other lobsters in a conflict. This liquid is made up of chemicals that signal the size, sex, mood, and strength of the lobster. Often the stronger, healthier, bigger lobster's signals win, and the other lobster backs off.

If both lobsters decide not to back off, then the conflict escalates to the next level, which involves advancing and retreating. If that continues, and one lobster does not back off, then it is full combat. Using their claws, they attack and try to flip the other lobster on its back. If neither is successful, then the conflict proceeds to full-on attack, with serious damage dealt and sometimes fatal endings.

The outcome of this conflict changes the chemicals in the brain. The winner produces more serotonin and less octopamine, which makes the lobster "cocky" and less likely to back down. The winner will strut. Why? Because more serotonin helps to regulate postural flexion. A winner stands taller, more upright, signaling the win physically. As Peterson states, "High serotonin/low octopamine characterizes the winner."[48] The opposite ratio of high octopamine and low serotonin characterizes the loser.

The winning lobster then establishes dominance by intimidating any others who attempt to enter into conflict. As female lobsters mature, they seek the dominant male lobsters with which to mate. Females do this through spraying appealing scents and aphrodisiacs. (Female lobsters will fight during the maternal cycle.)

However, in the research, it is not enough to be the strongest, most dominant male. One dominant male can be taken down by two males of lesser strength. In the study of primates, "males who stay on top longer are those who form reciprocal coalitions with their lower-status compatriots, and who pay careful attention to the troupe's females and their infants."[49]

The lobster male and female dance of dominance, status, and position plays itself out with human adolescents. Adolescence is literally one of the first forays into that dance. It shows up in middle and high school awkwardly and painfully for many students. Peterson goes on to say this: "Low-ranking lobsters produced comparatively low levels of serotonin. This is also true of low-ranking human beings, and those low levels decrease more with each defeat. Low serotonin means decreased confidence…more response to stress…less happiness…more pain and anxiety, more illness, and a shorter lifespan."[50]

This need for dominance is one of the reasons for bullying. In the research, females tend to bully individuals they know, and they are more popular if they bully. Males tend to bully individuals they do not know, and they tend to be less liked. In both males and females, those at the very top level of the social structure and those at the very bottom of the social structure tend not to bully. Among females, the bullies tend to be at the level right below the top.

The "mating dance" comes out of puberty and the development of sexual identity.

Sex and Gender and Identity

Biologically, sex differences are determined by the gametes (sex cells). Males have small, mobile gametes (sperm), and females have larger, immobile gametes (eggs). Sexual differences include the presence or absence of a Y chromosome, the gonads (ovaries or testes), sex hormone balances (estrogen, testosterone), external genitalia, and anatomy of reproduction (uterus or prostate). Males and females each have 46 chromosomes. While most individuals are familiar with the XX and XY chromosomes, there are other combinations such as XXY, XXXY, etc. Individuals who have mixed sexual anatomy are intersex.[51]

In terms of gender identity, if the assigned sex and the psychological experience differ, then the individual may identify as transgender, transsexual, or nonbinary.

Sexual identities (which are distinct from but related to gender identities) can include heterosexuality (attraction to opposite sex), bisexuality (attraction to both sexes), homosexuality (attraction to same sex), asexual (lack of attraction or interest), and pansexuality (attraction regardless of sex or gender identity).

Production of Sperm and Eggs

The male body produces fresh sperm every day and continues that throughout most of the life span.

> Your testicles are constantly producing new sperm in spermatogenesis. The full process takes about 64 days. During spermatogenesis, your testicles make several million sperm per day—about 1,500 per second. By the end of a full sperm production cycle, you can regenerate up to 8 billion sperm. This may seem like overkill, but you release anywhere from 20 to 300 million sperm cells in a single milliliter of semen. Your body maintains a surplus to ensure there's a fresh supply for conception.[52]

Females, on the other hand, are born with all of their eggs and lose them as they age. "At birth, a baby girl has approximately from 700,000 to 2 million eggs (oocytes). Every single month of her life until she reaches puberty, she loses about 11,000 eggs. By the time she is in her teens, she has between 300,000-400,000 eggs, and fewer than 500 will be ovulated."[53]

The constant production of sperm impacts male realities. Males produce sperm daily. Testosterone production increases during adolescence.

> Testosterone is an important male hormone. A male begins to produce testosterone as early as seven weeks after conception. Testosterone levels rise during puberty, peak during the late teen years, and then level off. After age 30 or so, it's normal for a man's testosterone levels to decrease slightly every year.[54]

What Does Testosterone Do to Brain Development?

> Testosterone is…present in both sexes. And one of its roles is "in reorganizing the brain during adolescence," says [neuroscientist Anna] Tyborowska. It helps control how different brain structures develop during this time. Testosterone levels tend to climb in puberty. And those increases have been linked with how the adolescent brain performs… When forced to control their emotions, teens with less testosterone

tend to rely on their limbic systems, Tyborowska's group now finds. This makes their brain activity look more like that of younger children. Teens with higher testosterone, though, use their prefrontal cortex to rein in their emotions. Their brain activity includes the prefrontal cortex regulation of the deep-brain limbic system. This pattern looks more adult.[55]

Why Peers Become More Important in Adolescence Than Adults

The first time the brain organizes and structures itself is from birth to age six. The amygdala or emotional self is highly structured by the time a child is three years old. When a child goes through puberty, the brain is restructured again. The brain "prunes" itself, the hormones change, and sexual and gender identity play an incredible role in the development of the adolescent. This chart shows some of these changes.

	Birth to three	Adolescence
Bonding and attachment	Is to the primary caregiver(s)	Is to peers
Self-construction	As a child	As an emerging adult
Brain development	Basic structures	Prefrontal cortex, risk centers, reward analysis, planning
Adult involvement	Critical for survival	Critical for guidance, attunement, growth
Physical development	Physical body and use of it	Sexual body and use of it

Peers become the mirror through which the adolescent sees their self, and so peers take on an additional significance. While childhood was about learning to use the physical body, adolescence is now focused on the sexuality and gender of the adolescent.

Puberty alters appearances as well, as one's body changes, grows, and develops. Carl Pickhardt identifies these issues as adolescents go through puberty:

- Feeling vulnerable about body changes that are out of their control.
- Desiring more physical privacy.
- Awakening of sexual interests and fantasies—females go to romantic movies/novels, males to pornography.
- Increased self-evaluation.
- Preoccupation with social expectations and peer treatment.[56]

What Happens in the Brain as It Moves Through Puberty into Adulthood?

Puberty and the sexual, physical, chemical, and structural changes that occur then impact the ways in which adolescent brains develop and mature. The prefrontal cortex in adolescents is the last part of the brain to develop. The brain develops from the back to the front. This development finishes between ages 25 and 30.[57]

"While 95% of the human brain has developed by the age of six, scientists report that the greatest spurts of growth after infancy occur just around adolescence."[58]

Factors Influencing Brain Development in Adolescents

The following factors influence the maturation of the adolescent brain:

- Heredity and environment
- Sex hormones
- Physical, mental, economic, and psychological status
- Surgical interventions
- Sleep
- Nutritional status
- Pre- and postnatal insult
- Pharmacotherapy
- Drug abuse, nicotine, caffeine, alcohol, etc.
- Age (10–25 years)[59]

"MRI studies have suggested that neurocircuitry and myelinogenesis remain under construction during adolescence because these events in the CNS depend on sex hormones that are specifically increased during puberty."[60]

According to Jay Giedd,

The adolescent brain is not a broken or defective adult brain. It has been exquisitely forged by the forces of evolution to have different features compared to children or adults, but these differences have served our species well. The three most robust adolescent behavioral changes are (1) increased risk-taking; (2) increased sensation-seeking; and (3) a move away from parents toward greater peer affiliation. That these changes occur not only in humans, but in all social mammals, suggests a deeply rooted biology, which fosters independent functioning and separation from the natal family.[61]

Giedd goes on to say that after puberty, the brain matures by specialization, not by growing larger. The brain overproduces gray matter (volume peaks at 11 for females and 13 for males) and does selective elimination as it responds to environmental demands. The prefrontal cortex is that last area to mature.

White matter allows for greater myelination—which is rather like insulation for the dendrites—and allows for greater connectivity, multiprocessing, and integration of the brain and its parts. The myelin sheath covers the dendrites. (The thickness of the myelin sheath can be an indicator of intelligence.) The brain, as it integrates, will shed myelin that slows down new connections and decreases plasticity. "Plasticity" means that the brain can be adaptive and change. The reward circuitry of the brain is reformulated at this time. Sex hormones (estrogen, progesterone, and testosterone) play an important role in myelination.

The brain develops via overproduction of cells. In adolescence, it prunes and eliminates cells and develops specialization. "The human brain is a social brain."[62] Learning is a social activity. The brain is wired to interact and bond with others.

The corpus callosum is the thick cord of nerves that connects the two halves of the brain and seems to have a very genetic basis. In fact, in identical twins, it is almost alike. But the cerebellum, in the back of the brain, is very different in twins and seems to be heavily influenced by the environment. The cerebellum experiences the most change during adolescence. It is involved in the coordination of cognitive processes, as well as physical coordination. The more complicated the task, the more the cerebellum is involved.

Three neurotransmitters play a significant role in the development of adolescent behavior: dopamine, serotonin, and melatonin. Dopamine is involved in movement, emotional response, and the experience of pleasure and pain. During adolescence, dopamine production decreases, which can lead to mood swings and difficulty with appropriate emotional responses. Serotonin is involved with anxiety, arousal, and the control of impulses. Serotonin production also decreases in adolescence. Melatonin regulates sleep—circadian rhythms, waking and sleeping times. Melatonin production increases in adolescence, leading to the need for more sleep. In other words, serotonin and dopamine production decrease in adolescence—both of which help regulate emotional responses and behavior! And melatonin increases, which makes them want to sleep more. In fact, the circadian rhythm changes for many adolescents. They go to sleep later and wake later. In the book *Why We Sleep,* the author argues for later school start times.[63]

The white matter and gray matter volumes change in the part of the brain that is the social brain. Socialization becomes much more important. In addition, sex and other hormones activate neurocircuits that lead to the "development of sexual salience of sensory stimuli, sexual motivation, and expression of copulatory behavior."[64]

Reward Circuitry in the Brain and Sensation-Seeking

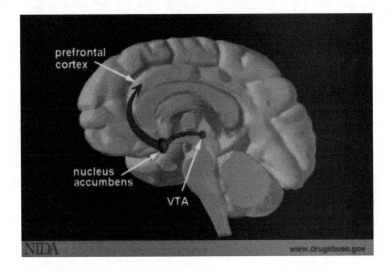

One pathway important to understanding the effects of drugs on the brain is called the reward pathway. The reward pathway involves several parts of the brain, some of which are highlighted in this image: the ventral tegmental area (VTA), the nucleus accumbens, and the prefrontal cortex. When activated by a rewarding stimulus (e.g., food, water, sex), information travels from the VTA to the nucleus accumbens and then up to the prefrontal cortex.[65]

The job of the reward pathway is to release chemicals that give you a rush of pleasure so that you will repeat a behavior. (In order to survive, your brain is hardwired to get you to repeat behaviors that are beneficial for you.) The message goes to your prefrontal cortex, which is the "command center" of the brain.

However, "the brain can be tricked. When addictive substances are used, they give the brain a 'false signal.' Since the brain can't tell the difference between the [addiction] and a real, healthy reward, it goes ahead and activates the reward center."[66] It does this by releasing dopamine, which makes the brain crave the fake reward. With more dopamine, the cravings get stronger.

Your brain shuts off a natural pleasure. "Dopamine cells stop firing after repeated consumption of a natural reward," states Nora Volkow.[67] But addictive substances continue to increase dopamine—there is no shutoff. The brain is tricked into unhealthy behavior. Eventually, the brain will "normalize" the experience, and then it takes increased amounts of the substance to get the same "high."

"In fact, most drug addictions initiate during adolescence, and early drug abuse is usually associated with an increased incidence of physical tolerance and dependence."[68]

Sensation-seeking can include addictions that may come in the form of drugs (including alcohol and nicotine), porn, screen time, sex, gambling, shopping, etc. The areas of the brain that govern impulse control (prefrontal cortex) and motivation and reward (nucleus accumbens) are not fully developed in adolescence.

Drugs/Substance Abuse

The research is fairly strong that substance abuse in adolescents is damaging because the brain is not fully matured. Cannabis is the substance most used by adolescents. "Epidemiological studies have suggested that adolescent cannabis abuse may increase their risk of developing cognitive abnormalities, psychotic illness, mood disorders, and other illicit substance abuse later in life…increas[ing] the risk of psychiatric disorders."[69]

Nicotine use increases the production of dopamine and leads to an increased vulnerability to nicotine use as an adult.

Alcohol is a toxin for the body. Increasingly, evidence indicates that long-lasting neurophysiological changes may occur in the brain with exposure to ethanol during adolescence. Differences in how males and females drink, abuse, and depend upon alcohol begin to emerge between late puberty and young adulthood. "A male predominance in overall drug abuse appears by the end of adolescence, while girls develop a rapid progression from the time of the first abuse to dependence; this represents female-based vulnerability."[70]

Porn

Porn has the same effect on the brain as drugs. Porn hijacks the amygdala and reward center. Just like with drugs, your brain builds a tolerance and requires more porn (and eventually harder-core porn) to get the same sensational effect. And just like a drug, giving up porn produces withdrawal symptoms.

The Numbers[71]

9 out of 10 Boys and 6 out of 10 girls will be exposed to pornography before the age of 18!

In the research on adolescent porn use, early conditioning is a huge factor in how the brain wires itself (remember, what fires together wires together) and the neural pathways that are established. Because the teen brain is malleable and still forming, one of the biggest issues with porn is that it establishes a relationship between the screen and sex—not between a human being and sex. "Porn can actually overpower the brain's natural ability to have real sex."[72] A chemical called DeltaFosB is released when the reward center gets activated, and it creates strong mental connections. DeltaFosB is key to learning any new skills but can lead to addictive behaviors—particularly in adolescents. It is referred to as "the molecular switch for addiction" because it switches on long-term cravings.[73]

In the research, excessive porn use often leads to erectile dysfunction (ED). What is very interesting is that if an individual gets into porn as an adult and is a healthy adult, then ED recovery from the porn addiction (called "rebooting") can occur around two months after the porn viewing stops. However, if the individual started viewing porn in adolescence and begins to have ED in the mid to late 20s, it takes 4–6 months for recovery from ED. The early conditioning is to the screen.

Porn changes attitudes about women. "In fact, a 2015 peer-reviewed research study that analyzed 22 different studies from seven different countries concluded that there is 'little doubt that, on the average, individuals who consume pornography more frequently are more likely to hold attitudes [supporting] sexual aggression and engage in actual acts of sexual aggression.'"[74]

In the research on "hypersexualized" females, researchers find there is a high correlation to watching porn. The research also found that a significant percentage of "hypersexualized" females also suffer from bipolar mental illness. What are "hypersexualized" adolescents and youths? "Various patterns of increased sexuality…that is excessive, developmentally precocious, compulsive, aggressive, or otherwise socially inappropriate…and is associated with a variety of factors…to include sexual abuse, physical abuse, life stress, impaired family relationships…PTSD…and possibly bipolar disorder."[75]

In adolescence, establishing neural pathways in the reward center related to sexual relationships through a screen leads to "damaged relationships, disappointment, and isolation."[76]

Screens

In 2010, adolescents in the U.S. spent 8½ hours (on average) per day on screens.[77]

Ninety-nine percent of males and 94% of females play video games. Video games stimulate and activate the reward center of the brain. As in all reward center (nucleus accumbens) activations, dopamine is increased.[78]

Social media sites are heavily used by adolescents. A large part of the brain is dedicated to social cognition.

Our ability to gauge the moods and intentions of others, to detect the truth or falsehood of their communications, to discern friend from foe, and to form alliances are amongst its most complex and important tasks…In fact, across primate species, the single best predictor of the size of the neocortex is the size of that species' social group.[79]

Will a dependence upon the screen versions of human interactions actually impede the ability of the adolescent to deal with real-life people and events? The research is not in.

Risk-Taking Behavior

"Risk-taking behavior is a normal and necessary component of adolescence."[80] Risk-taking is one way that an individual can have new experiences and discover new talents and aspects of the self. The nerve fibers connecting the right and left sides of the brain are maturing.

In the research, by the time adolescents are 15, their ability to make decisions related to a hypothetical situation are equal to an adult's. However, teens will still engage in risky behaviors, even when they understand the risks. Risk-taking behavior increases if there are three or more teens present. Interestingly, teens tend not to engage in risky behavior when they are by themselves or with one other teen. But in groups of three teens or more, the risk-taking behavior jumps. Researchers have identified "hot cognition" (intense feelings and arousal) and "cold cognition" (critical and overanalyzing). Teens tend to make better decisions in cold-cognition situations. When the situation has overlays of social rejection or acceptance, then teens often make risky decisions. Adolescent brains tend to overemphasize the positive and downplay the negative aspects of the risk. The amygdala, prefrontal cortex, and limbic system are still in development.

This is exacerbated by the adolescent fantasy of being a huge hero who is invincible and cannot die. The risks do not apply to them. It won't happen to them. It might happen to someone else, but not to them.

Leading Causes of Death Among Adolescents

The following are the main ways adolescents aged 10–24 die:

- Sexually transmitted infections (19 million diagnosed every year)
  - In 2004, 39% of adolescents ages 15–24 engaged in unprotected sex

- Motor vehicle crashes (30%)
  - Of the 30% involved in crashes, 41% were linked to deaths

- Homicide (15%)

- Suicide (12%)[81]

"Injury and violence are the two most common leading causes of death during adolescence."[82]

Prefrontal Cortex, Social Cognition, and Moral Development

Part of what happens in adolescence is the development of a moral code, and this is a key function of the prefrontal cortex. Development of a moral code is also a key player in the regulation of behavior.

Schools underestimate the importance of the development of social cognition.

Social cognition "is a broad term used to describe cognitive processes related to the perception, understanding, and implementation of linguistic, auditory, visual, and physical cues that communicate emotional and interpersonal information."[83]

> Changes in social behavior are driven by both social and biological factors. During adolescence, it is likely that peer interactions and societal influences, as well as genetically determined hormonal milieus, influence social behavior. However, since the recent discovery that the brain matures considerably during adolescence, evidence has emerged pointing to the role of neural maturation in the development of social cognition during adolescence.[84]

Social information processing involves three interacting neural nodes that identify and find social stimuli, which are then put in a larger integrated cognitive and emotional construct. These three are (1) the "detection node"—

figures out social meaning from body cues, (2) the "affective node"—involves the amygdala and limbic system to identify the emotional meanings, and (3) the "cognitive regulatory node"—the prefrontal cortex and its role in determining impulse inhibition, cognitive frame of meaning, and behavior.

In adolescence, social cognition includes the development of the imaginary audience, perspective-taking, and executive functioning.

Imaginary Audience

"The emergence of the social self seems to be marked by a period of heightened self-consciousness, during which adolescents are thought to become increasingly preoccupied with other people's concerns about their actions, thoughts, and appearance."[85]

> This adolescent egocentrism causes most adolescents to have an inflated, even melodramatic, view of themselves, their significance, and their role in the world. They feel as though no one has their problems (including self-esteem problems) and that they are unique. Elkind (1967) identifies several aspects of adolescent egocentrism to include the *personal fable* (the belief that [the adolescent] will be famous, adored, worshiped, legendary) and the *invincibility fable* (regardless of [the adolescent's] behavior, no harm will occur)…Young adolescent[s'] egocentrism causes [them] to create an "imaginary audience," who watches, critiques, and pays attention to everything the individual does (Berger, 2011, p. 409). This imaginary audience makes the adolescent even more self-conscious. What this audience does more than anything else is *judge* the adolescent—and so, during the day, any incident, innocuous or with intent, impacts the adolescent either for better or for worse—"Oh, he looked at me" (interpretation: *I must be beautiful*) or "Oh, he ignored me" (interpretation: *I must be ugly*). The imaginary audience obscures any reality checks. The adolescent, therefore, literally careens through the day in response to this imaginary audience. This self-absorbed psychological experience feeds into and helps develop adolescent identity.[86]

Perspective-Taking

Perspective-taking means "the ability to take another's perspective [and] is crucial for successful social communication. Reasoning about others, and understanding what they think, feel, or believe, involves stepping into their 'mental shoes' and taking their perspective."[87]

In other words, can the adolescent view the situation from not only their own perspective, but from someone else's perspective as well? This is key in the development of beneficial behavior because it builds compassion and social cognition.

When my son was in the ninth grade, he came home from school very upset. One of the seniors had committed suicide because he had found out that his girlfriend was pregnant. The senior boy came from a very strict religious family. My son was outraged. He said, "How could he leave the girl and his baby alone? How could he leave them without his support? What a coward he is."

This would be an example of perspective-taking—not looking at a situation through your own eyes but through those of another person.

Perspective-taking eventually leads to a moral code.

The Development of a Moral Code

Why is development of a moral code even important? Because all decision-making is based upon a belief system. What is wrong? What is right? What is best for me? What is best for someone else? How do I balance my individual needs with the needs of the group? In whose best interest do I operate? Is there a compromise available?

The following graphic was developed by Jen Nehl, based on work by Jack M. Jose.[89]

Kohlberg's Model of Moral Development

Postconventional Morality

Stage 6

Universal Ethical Principles

(What if everybody did that? World shaped view by doing what is right for everyone.)

"I couldn't live with myself if I let them die."

Stage 5

Social Contract Orientation

(It's the consensus of thoughtful people. Recognize the difference between morals and laws.)

"I couldn't face the community if I let my wife die."

Conventional Morality

Stage 4

Law and Order Orientation

(Do your duty. Prosocial obedience.)

"Saving my wife's life is more important than protecting my car."

Stage 3

Good Boy, Good Girl

(Do it for me. Good behavior conforms to good intentions.)

"You *should* do it for me *because* you love me."

Preconventional Morality

Stage 2

Instrumental-Relativism Orientation

(If it feels good, do it! Seek reward, follow hidden rules.)

"You're worth my time *only* because you are nice and pretty."

Stage 1

Punishment and Obedience Orientation

(It's okay as long as you don't get caught. Avoid punishment; be obedient.)

"If I lie well enough or am sneaky enough, I won't get caught. And if I do get caught, it doesn't matter because I know someone who can get me out of trouble."

A moral code always shows up in "should/should not" or "ought/ought not" messages.

What follows is a story that illustrates how a moral code is a part of everyday situations at school. It also illustrates that the development of perspective-taking is evidenced by the principal, not the other adults nor the student. Neither the student nor other adults, except for the principal, are able to see the perspective of the other.

A Story: Enforce Consequences, but Change the Approach

Written by Michael Curl, a middle school principal in Texas

Stepping into the role of middle school principal from high school assistant principal brought many new experiences. One of the most surprising was stepping into lunch duty with more than 300 middle school students. Today was especially interesting, as when I stepped in, I saw an assistant principal, security officer, and police officer forming a half-circle around a sixth-grade female student who was sitting and crying. She was visibly upset and had tears streaming down her face. I'd seen the young girl before, but never under these circumstances. Rarely did I see her in the office, but I recognized her from pre-AP class visits.

When I asked what the problem was (as there wasn't an obvious violation of the student code of conduct occurring at the moment), I was told that she wouldn't move. Not that she was cursing, causing a disruption, or presenting a danger to herself or others. She wouldn't move. Something occurred earlier that caused the assistant principal to request that the student move her seat. The student, gifted academically, stated that she was not the cause of the issue that was being addressed and didn't understand why she had to move. She was adamant that she wasn't the cause and was not going to move based on the behaviors of others.

As with many gifted students, she had a strong sense of justice and moral concern. Starting from an early age, many gifted children show evidence of advanced sensitivity about moral concerns in their empathy for others, compassionate responses to the plight of others, idealism, concern about world issues, and their advanced understanding and judgment of moral issues.[90] Her fight-or-flight response had kicked in, and her version of the fight was "I did nothing wrong and shouldn't have to do anything other than finish my lunch."

What was not known was the emotional dance that was occurring behind the mask of this upset student. I asked the police officer, security officer, and administrator to step away as I spoke with the student. After I heard her plight, she got up and walked with me outside, up and down the bus landing. Utilizing calming techniques such as looking up, drinking water, and deep breathing, we were able to get to a point where the crying and raised voice had subsided.

This situation was a prime example of consequences always being needed and an approach that needed changing. This incident was a game changer for our campus as it demonstrated the need for training on several things that could have kept this situation from escalating to the point where an academically solid student ends up in crisis because of the actions of the adults charged with her care. Could she have reacted differently and just accepted the consequence for something she didn't do? Yes, she could have. But as the leader of the campus, I did not see this as a binary situation. It did not have to be "do what I say or you end up in tears." With proper training and dialogue, our team would be better equipped to deal with the emotional realities that were present on our campus.

A moral code is a part of executive functioning.

Executive Functioning

Executive functioning includes the following: control and coordination of thoughts and behaviors, inhibitory control, processing speed, prospective memory, working memory, decision-making, and risk-taking. All of these are related to the development of the prefrontal cortex.[91]

Processing speed is related to IQ and the myelin sheath that covers the axons (cortical thickness).

What Can You Do to Help Adolescents Have Beneficial Brain Development?

1. **Embrace the development of social cognition.** Schools often deny, negate, suppress, or ignore the development of social cognition, even though it is a critical piece of development for this age. I know one high school principal who did this: She wanted to improve attendance rates, reduce tardies, and increase achievement, so she built in a 20-minute time frame, right after first period, for socialization. Students could have that time to socialize if they had a certain attendance percentage, few tardies, and passing grades. They could meet with friends, use their phones, and socialize. Students who did not meet the criteria worked with teachers to improve achievement.

2. **Understand differences in the development of social cognition.** Females tend to develop social cognition through conversation. Males tend to do it through shared activities.

3. **Use advisory periods to develop perspective-taking.** Perspective-taking is such a critical part of social cognitive development in adolescents that it is worth devoting advisory periods to developing it.

4. **Encourage nutrition that includes fish oils and fatty acids, which support beneficial brain development (adolescent brain maturation).** Eating fresh fish and oils high in omega-3 fatty acids supports adolescent brain development. Sources include nuts, flaxseed, fruits, vegetable oils, mackerel, anchovies, sardines, and animal fats. White matter abnormalities and myelination integrity are linked to depression and other mental illnesses. In one research study, the depressed participants significantly alleviated their depression by taking fish oils and fatty acids. "Major depressive disorder (MDD) is one of the top five causes of disability worldwide, with a lifetime prevalence of approximately 10–18%."[92]

5. **Encourage sleep—at least eight hours a night.** Why? In the article "Our (Mother's) Mitochondria and Our Mind," the authors explain that mitochondria come only from your mother. Mitochondria are in every cell of your body. They are organelles that take the food you eat (glucose) and the air you breathe (oxygen) and give you energy. In this process, waste is created—free radicals, carbon dioxide, etc. When you sleep, brain cells shrink by 60%, and that allows the fluid pathways in the brain to enlarge. While you sleep, your brain disposes of waste through the widened passages. When mitochondria are healthy, they look tubular in a microscope; when they are partially contaminated, they look like donuts; and when they are full of contaminants, they look like a blob. When the mitochondria are dead, so is the cell. Researchers are now tracking many emotional issues—such as depression, etc.—to damaged mitochondria. The other reason for sleep is that the brain does a lot of reorganizing of the previous day's experiences, brain cleaning, etc. Interestingly enough, the last two hours of sleep (between hours six and eight) are the most important for this to occur.[93]

6. **Understand that the development of the male brain lags behind the development of the female brain.**

    The male brain is about 10% larger than the female brain across all the stages of…3 to 20; not to imply that the increased size implies any sort of advantage, because it doesn't. The IQs are very similar. But there are differences between the boy and girl brains, both in the size of certain structures and in their developmental path. The basal ganglia, which are a part of the brain that helps the frontal lobe do executive functioning, are larger in females, and this is a part of the brain that is often smaller in the childhood illnesses I mentioned, such as ADD and Tourette syndrome…But in the general trend for brain maturation, it's that girls' brains mature earlier than boys' brains.[94]

7. **Use curriculum and instructional approaches that involve social interaction.** Project-based learning is a good approach to use.

8. **Share information with students about developing social cognition.** During an advisory period, use the PBS *Frontline* episode "Inside the Teenage Brain" to teach adolescents what is happening to them during this time of development.

9. Share coping strategies with students. Give students strategies for dealing with cyberbullying, for example.

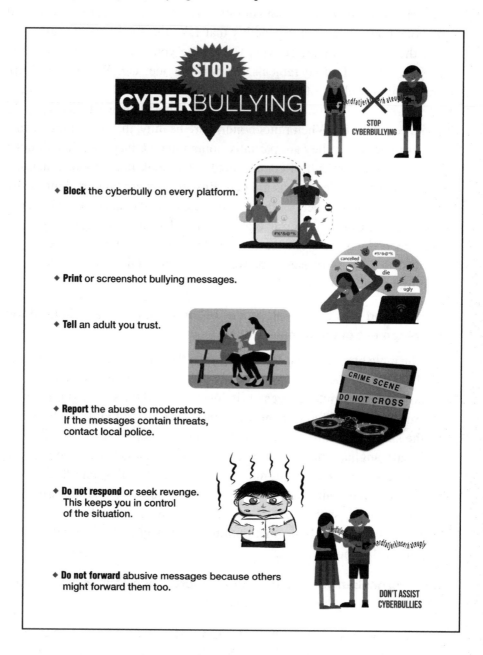

10. **Understand the modus operandi (MO) of instigators.** Instigators are those students who consistently create issues. One secondary school I know had the teachers take video of student fights. It was almost always the same group of students who were watching the fights. They are the instigators, and they have an MO. The parts of the MO are that it involves a statement that is partially true, it usually contains a sexual innuendo, and it almost always involves some verbal baiting.

11. **Work on perspective-taking with girls who are angry, belligerent, and treat their peers poorly.** One of the characteristics of many of these girls is that their relationship with their father is either nonexistent or not good. A secondary counselor once asked me why some girls are attracted to "bad boys." I told him to ask them about the relationship they have with their father.

Because the emotional part of the brain is structured before there is language to assign to experiences, individuals record what is "normal." If you are never able to get the attention of your father, if he is absent emotionally or physically or is deceased, the translation to a young mind is often "I wasn't enough. What is wrong with me?" This is what Daniel J. Siegel says about it in his book *Mindsight:*

> If we are not seen, if our caregivers do not attune to us, and we are met with the experience of feeling invisible or misunderstood, our nervous system responds with a sudden activation of the brake portion of its regulatory circuits. Slamming on the brakes creates a distinctive physiological response: heaviness in the chest, nausea in the belly, and downcast or turned-away eyes. We literally shrink into ourselves from a pain that is often beneath our awareness...It is experienced as a state of shame...Shame states are common in children whose parents are repeatedly unavailable or who habitually fail to attune to them. When shame from nonattuned communication is combined with parental hostility, toxic humiliation ensues... The shame gets translated to "I am bad." It is better for the child to feel defective than to realize his/her attachment figures are untrustworthy and dangerous.[95]

Chapter Summary

1. Puberty changes the brain by restructuring, in part because of hormonal changes.

2. During puberty, the brain reorganizes from the back of the brain to the front. The last part to develop is the prefrontal cortex.

3. Sensation-seeking and risk-taking parts of the brain develop before the prefrontal cortex.

4. Two critical issues the brain is concerned with are the development of social cognition and perspective-taking. Adolescents work very hard to develop both. Schools often ignore these developmental needs.

5. The reward center (pleasure center) of the brain is active. Drugs, porn, and screen time can all impact how the brain rewires at this time.

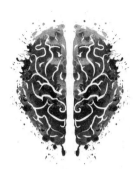

The 4 Hippocampus

Your memory and the stories you
carry in your head—identity

> **"My experiences trump your truth."**
> –Dr. Rickey Frierson
>
> **"The universe is made up of stories, not of atoms."**
> –Muriel Rukeyser[96]

The Hippocampus

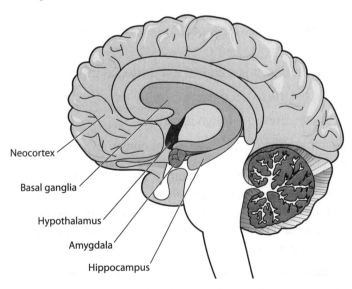

Neocortex

Basal ganglia

Hypothalamus

Amygdala

Hippocampus

The hippocampus is the part of the brain where we keep our memories and stories
of who we are.

Scientists have long known that recording a memory requires adjusting the connections between neurons. Each memory tweaks some tiny subset of the neurons in the brain (the human brain has 100 billion neurons in all), changing the way they communicate. Neurons send messages to one another across narrow gaps called synapses. A synapse is like a bustling port, complete with machinery for sending and receiving cargo—neurotransmitters, specialized chemicals that convey signals between neurons. All of the shipping machinery is built from proteins, the basic building blocks of cells...Eric Kandel [is] a neuroscientist at Columbia University in New York City. In five decades of research, Kandel has shown how short-term memories— those lasting a few minutes—involve relatively quick and simple chemical changes to the synapse that make it work more efficiently. Kandel, who won a share of the 2000 Nobel Prize in Physiology or Medicine, found that to build a memory that lasts hours, days, or years, neurons must manufacture new proteins and expand the docks, as it were, to make the neurotransmitter traffic run more efficiently. Long-term memories must literally be built into the brain's synapses.[97]

From these long-term memories, we in part construct the "story" of who we are. Early childhood and adolescent experiences create internal stories and responses. As a group of researchers led by Kate McLean at Western Washington University states, "The stories we tell about ourselves reveal ourselves, construct ourselves, and sustain ourselves through time."[98] We act on those stories.

As McLean states, the following aspects of these long-term memories contribute to our story:

1. Identity development is a crucial psychosocial task.

2. Identity is constructed, it does not simply arise.

3. Identity is constructed through narrative.

4. And most importantly...identity is not constructed alone.[99]

Just as there are the "big five" personality traits that are universal (neuroticism/ less neurotic, openness to experience/less open to experience, extraversion/ introversion, agreeableness/less agreeable, and conscientious/less conscientious), there is growing awareness that there are the "big three" key features of internal stories. These big three are:

1. **Motivational and affective themes:** (a) How much autonomy and connection is there? (b) What is the ratio of positive to negative stories? (c) Are the stories dominated by good situations turning bad or bad situations working out well in the end?

2. **Autobiographical reasoning:** (a) How much do we think about our stories? (b) Can we extrapolate meaning? (c) Can we see links between key events? (d) Can we identify ways in which we have and have not changed?

3. **Structure:** How much do our stories make sense, and are they coherent in terms of the timeline, the context, and the facts?

People who have no connection between the past and the now, no sense of the future—e.g., who they were, who they are, and who they will be—are associated in the research with suicidal ideation and are prone to alcoholism, violent youth offenses, depression, and mental illness. "In fact, many of the conflicts in the world, from simple road rage to outright war, can be seen as stemming from fractured identities."[100]

With the loss of the immediate and extended family and religious and cultural traditions, the questioning of authority and adults, travel, moving, lack of stable neighborhoods, and with so many outside sources influencing identity formation (media), the ability to have a coherent sense of self is very difficult. "The existential angst that comes from the emptiness, meaninglessness, disconnection, and fluidity of modern society creates a need for 'identity work.'"[101] Psychotherapy, consumerism, and the distraction of entertainment have attempted to fill that need, but they have not been very effective, and in some cases have made things worse.

"Narrative ecology of self" refers to a compilation of stories that a person hears and sees (and sometimes is not told), the stories others tell of that person, and the social context of the stories.

This is McLean's model of narrative ecology of self.[102]

Identity is held in the stories we tell ourselves about ourselves, in the stories others tell about us, and in the stories our culture tells.

Questions You Can Ask Students

1. If you met someone new for the first time, what story would you tell them about yourself?

2. What is a story your mother (caregiver, grandmother, father) tells about you?

3. Can you tell me about something that happened to you in grades K–3? In grades 4–8? In high school?

4. Who is a person you have known your entire life and who knows you? Do you care about them?

5. How much freedom do you have to make your own choices? Use a scale of 1 (never) to 10 (always).

6. When you think about your life, do you have more happy stories or more sad stories?

7. Have you had bad things in your life turn out for the best?

8. How are you the same as you were five years ago? How are you different?

9. Did anything that happened in elementary school help you with high school?

10. What is something you will remember forever?

11. In what ways are you different than the movies and social media like Instagram and Snapchat say you should be?

What These Questions Mean

Question 1: Identifies basic parts of identity. What do they identify as important to know?

Question 2: Stories other people tell about us—particularly our caregiver—are crucial in forming identity.

Question 3: Does their story make sense over time?

Question 4: How solid are their connections and belonging over time?

Question 5: Autonomy is key in allowing someone to determine identity.

Question 6: The ratio of good to bad stories forms identity.

Question 7: Can you take a "bad" event and make it into something good? This is critical for integration and personal growth.

Question 8: Coherence and continuity over time.

Question 9: Integration of past into present.

Question 10: Defining moment. Usually a disruption and crisis point. Almost always motivates change.

Question 11: Can you integrate culturally and have a sense of who you are?

What follow are two stories—one in which a student is able to construct a coherent internal story and one in which a student is not able to construct a coherent internal story.

A Story: Lamar

Written by Norma Vijeila, principal of an alternative school in California

Lamar is a polite and friendly 16-year-old young man. He is always respectful towards students and staff. He has a smile and warm kindness that can be felt when he comes to school happy. Lamar had envisioned a bright future for himself. He was exploring attending trade school after graduation with a goal of getting a job that would allow him to support himself. But in the last six months, Lamar's behavior has taken a drastic change.

A security guard who saw Lamar bang his head against a wall in the hallway after exiting one of the classrooms reported the first occurrence. The security guard notified the administrator of the incident. The counselor followed up with Lamar, and Lamar did not provide details but said he would not do that again. A second incident was reported by security and other office staff who had seen Lamar storm out of a classroom. This time Lamar did not bang his head on the wall; instead, he punched the wall several times. When we followed up on this incident, Lamar did not provide details or reasons for punching the wall. We followed up with one of his teachers to find out what had made him so angry. His teacher told us that Lamar had written a note to a girl. In the note, he told the girl he liked her. When the girl read the note, she told him nicely that she did not like him like that. Lamar had kept his cool, but when it was time for him to go home for the day, he stormed out.

Before the Thanksgiving break, Lamar came to school carrying his backpack and a black trash bag containing his belongings. He asked the front-office staff to hold his bag while he was in class. He also told them that he was now homeless and would need to find a place to sleep. He gave vague details of a fight he had had with his mom that resulted in his mom kicking him out of the home. The front-office staff notified the counselor and the administrators of Lamar's situation. The counselor called the mom to notify her and to find out if indeed Lamar was homeless and in need of a shelter. Mom told the counselor that there had been a fight and that she had asked Lamar to leave, but she said Lamar could come home if he was willing to apologize. Lamar was counseled to apologize and return home.

A few weeks after the winter break, Lamar arrived with his right hand wrapped in bandages and bleeding. He asked the front office if he could use their phone to call his dad. After hanging up the phone, he called 911 and provided details of his injuries. After Lamar hung up the phone, I asked him to come to sit with me in another office so we could wait for the paramedics. I asked Lamar two questions: (1) Are you okay? and (2) Did you hurt anyone?

Lamar told me he had woken up late because his alarm did not work that morning. He wanted to take a shower, but since he was up late, his younger brother was already in the shower. Lamar asked his younger siblings to hurry up so he could have a turn to take a shower too. His mom interceded and told Lamar that he was late for the shower and he would have to do without one. This triggered his anger, and he began to hit the wall and the picture frames on the wall. His mom again kicked him out of the house and told him she would call police if he came back.

Once the paramedics arrived, we called Lamar's mom to notify her that Lamar was going to be taken to the hospital. However, his mom and all the other emergency contacts on Lamar's list did not answer our call. The school counselor and I ended up going to the hospital with Lamar. The school psychologist, who also was concerned for Lamar's well-being, came to see him at the hospital.

The hospital requested that a school administrator accompany Lamar while he was being treated. I sat by his side and began to ask Lamar questions about his relationship with his mom.

Lamar told me that he had been born to a crack addict. He spent his first five months in the hospital and then was adopted by his biological father's sister and her husband. He had never met his biological mother. His biological father had spent time incarcerated and had been released recently. Two years ago, his adoptive mom had divorced and was now engaged to remarry. Lamar had a good relationship with his adoptive dad, but when he moved out during the divorce, his adoptive dad told him he could not take Lamar with him because he was not his real dad. Six months ago, Lamar's mom's new boyfriend had moved in, and they decided Lamar could no longer stay with their family. Lamar's mom told Lamar she would look into returning him back to foster care since she did not want to deal with him anymore. Lamar had a good relationship with his biological dad, but he could not take Lamar in since he was couch surfing and not able to secure a job because of his criminal record.

Lamar ended up getting stitches in his hand and coming back to school, and we had to wait all day for a call back from a parent who would take responsibility for ensuring Lamar had a safe place to spend the night. Lamar's mom gave us permission to release Lamar to his biological dad until they could figure out a better placement for him. It has been a few months, and Lamar still does not have a place to call home. Multiple times we have contacted child protective services and the local authorities, and they have yet to figure out an outcome for Lamar's situation.

A Story: Maria

Written by Norma Vijeila, principal of an alternative school in California

Maria is a first-generation Mexican American. Her parents came from Mexico before she was born. Both parents are in the country illegally and do not speak much English. Maria has one younger brother seven years younger than her. She has grown up in an apartment where space has to be shared by multiple families. Her mom works 12-hour days, six days a week. Maria did well when she was in elementary school and middle school. As she transitioned to high school, her mom noticed a change in her behavior and her outlook towards her future.

At school, Maria had always been distant from everyone. She had a mean look on her face to prevent anyone from getting close to her. She always wore oversized sweatshirts and loose sweatpants. She sat in silence, not wanting to talk to anyone.

I met Maria when a fight erupted between two male students. Maria was at the center of this fight. According to the details we gathered, Maria was being accused of sending nude pictures of herself to a male student. Her boyfriend had never actually seen the pictures but accused Maria of sending them to the other male. He confronted the student and consequently wanted to fight him. Luckily, the staff was able to prevent the two boys from actually engaging in a physical altercation. When questioned, Maria denied that there had been any pictures and said that the other male had started the fight.

A few weeks later, Maria arrived at school with a cast on her right foot. Maria said she had fallen while she was horse-playing with her boyfriend. I called Maria's mom to ask about the injury, and her mom said that was the same story Maria told her. Her mom had taken Maria to the hospital, and she had to get a cast and seven screws to repair her ankle. Maria stood by her story. Later, Maria started missing many days of school. Her mom told us that Maria had been refusing to get out of bed for days. She always claimed she had cramps and could not get out of bed. Maria was doing poorly in school because she was missing so many days.

One day Maria came to school wearing jeans instead of her typical oversized sweatpants. The security guard told me he suspected that Maria had a weapon in her back pocket. I went and asked Maria to come to my office, and she indeed had a small pocketknife in her back pocket. I asked Maria why she was carrying a knife, and she said she needed it for self-defense since she had been jumped on her way to school a few weeks ago. We had to proceed with a suspension. Maria's mom attended the suspension meeting.

After the meeting, Maria asked to speak to me without her mom being present. Maria's mom agreed to leave the room. When she left the room, Maria disclosed that she had actually planned to use the pocketknife to end her life because she was going through so much that she just couldn't handle life anymore. She did not share many details with me, but she told me that she had recently discovered that her dad was cheating on her mom. Her dad had always been abusive towards her mom, and since Maria had told her mom that she knew of another woman, her mom had kicked her dad out of the house. Maria said she was depressed because of their living situation and not having money to pay the rent and buy food. I immediately contacted the team to assess Maria. It was determined that she was not a high risk for suicide but should definitely seek further support and attention. All along her mom said she did not believe Maria was suicidal; instead, she thought Maria was making excuses for not wanting to get her act together.

I have been following up with Maria for 18 months. I have collaborated with her teachers to motivate her to graduate. She is very close to graduation now. She moved out of her mom's house and says she has a better relationship with her mom. She does not see her dad often since he moved away. She is no longer in a relationship with the boy who accused her of sharing nude photos. She recently disclosed that he had pushed her so hard one time that it resulted in her broken ankle. Other times she could not get out of bed because he had beaten her so badly that she could not even stand. She was afraid to press charges against him because he threatened to get her parents deported, and then he would be the only person she would have in this country. She said that the abuse had gotten so bad that he would hit her in public places, not caring who saw him do it. Right now, Maria does not know what happened to him. She broke up with him, and he harassed her for a few weeks, and then he disappeared completely. No one in the neighborhood knew where he was.

Maria is hopeful that she will graduate high school and move on to college. At school, she still keeps to herself and does not want to disclose much of her personal story. She would like to be a first-generation college graduate so she can help her mom overcome poverty. She also hopes to one day be able to help her get citizenship in this country. I see amazing potential in Maria. She has given me permission to continue to mentor her and support her after high school. She would like to invite me to her college graduation, and I am looking forward to that day.

How Do You Help a Student Construct a Coherent Internal Story?

Over time	Who am I? What will stay the same about me and my character?	
Elementary school	Now	Future

In different settings		
At school	With friends	At home

Wounds

Everyone has wounds. Does your wound define you, or is it a part of you? If it defines you, your growth stagnates. If it becomes a part of you, your growth accelerates. If you have ever met someone who got a divorce 20 years ago and is still is bitter and angry, you have someone who has defined their life by a wound.

I have met individuals who have been so wounded by an issue or person or event that it defines them for the rest of their life. It may have been a death, divorce, an injury based on racial or gender identity, an illness, etc.

"Disruption is when narrative is most useful. When something unexpectedly happens, something challenging, we need a story."[103]

Here are nine of the most common kinds of wounds. The possible cause of the behavior is also identified.[104]

Childhood experience message/story/ wound	May cause this emotion and behavior	What they want from you
Environment emphasized that one must be good and correct. Do not make mistakes. The world is black and white—right or wrong. Competition to be the best.	Anger at self. Want to be perfect. Resent those who do not follow the rules.	Neatness and order. All the details. Clarify the criteria. Establish that perfection is not necessarily the goal.
Environment taught them that having or expressing their own needs leads to humiliation or rejection. Work to adapt to the needs of others in their environment.	Driven by feelings/heart. Focus on others' feelings rather than their own.	Help them limit what they say yes to doing. Have them identify their own feelings. Help them identify what they need in a situation.
Environment where they were valued and rewarded for getting things done. Don't believe that they can be loved if they are not productive. Child may take on parenting roles.	Ignore feelings—focus on tasks.	Opportunities for leadership. Identify the end result, and let them do the work. Ask them to identify what they sacrifice in their pursuit of achievement. What has value in their life aside from achievement?
Early environment in which they felt different and misunderstood by their parents, siblings, and peers. Lots of "what if?" Feel as if something is always missing.	Focus on their own feelings. They are their feelings.	Want to be recognized as unique and different. Want to be creative. Identify realistic situations as opposed to idealistic situations.
Often felt invisible as a child. Grew up either with an intrusive parent or a lack of deep, meaningful interactions with caregivers. Retreat to the world of thoughts. To survive, need to detach emotionally and hide.	Fear is outside of them. Focus on facts/ information and research.	Understand their need for solitude, exploration of the unknown, undiscovered. Want time for their projects. Do not want to feel uninformed or ignorant, to be "managed." Value autonomy and self-containment.

(continued on next page)

(continued from previous page)

Childhood experience message/story/wound	May cause this emotion and behavior	What they want from you
Often, not always, something unpredictable about early childhood environment. Learned there is always something to worry about.	Fear is internal. I am afraid for me.	Want to have security, belonging, predictability. Want to eliminate threats as much as possible.
In developmental years, the message was "You're on your own. Little support here." Create their own nirvana.	Ignores fear. Trades fear for experiences—the next adventure.	Want to maintain freedom and happiness, lots of variety, be excited and occupied, and avoid pain. Do not want to feel trapped, bored, or guilty.
Loss of childhood innocence or other experience that required them to take responsibility for self and others. Unstable environments or backgrounds where toughness was rewarded or bullied at school.	Direct anger at others. Arguing is intimacy and connection. Intense energy—all or nothing. Do not try to control me.	Challenge them right back. Tell them the truth—don't sugarcoat it. Let them have some sort of control over the situation—offer choices. Appeal to their soft side.
Grew up in environments where they felt unimportant and that their opinions and wants did not matter much.	Denies their anger. Tries to get everyone to get along. Tunes out and withdraws to a safe place.	Like structure, predictability, routines. Like to be part of a group with good relationships. Don't want conflict or stress.

A Story: Marquel

Written by Marye Jane Brockinton

Marquel transferred into my school as an overaged, under-credited junior in high school. He enrolled himself one week after school started. As the counselor and I began talking with him to create a class schedule, all Marquel talked about was joining the football team. After some investigation, we found Marquel did not have the number of credits nor the state-required grade level to participate. When the counselor shared the disappointing news, Marquel jumped out of the chair, yelled obscenities, and left, slamming the door of the office. Security heard and noticed his behavior. The security officer used calm words to ask Marquel what the problem was. Marquel began the obscenity-laced rant again. All of this happened within the first 30 minutes of his arrival on campus.

I found him down the hall, so I grabbed a water and encouraged him to give me a chance to figure something out for him. After he calmed, Marquel offered that his mother kicked him out of his home in another state. His uncle sent him money for a bus ticket to come live with him. I could tell he had developed a relationship with his uncle. Marquel said, "He got me. No one ever got me like him." The past tense caught my attention, so I asked where the uncle was now. Marquel began sobbing, stating the uncle had died of a heart attack three weeks earlier. Instantly, the tears stopped, and anger covered his face. "I don't need anyone," he said. The uncle's daughter was allowing Marquel to live with her. She was in her early 20s and working two jobs.

The football coach agreed to have Marquel as a manager and allowed him to work out with the team until he achieved the credits and GPA needed to play. In addition, the counselor developed a schedule that would allow Marquel to complete missing credits while also completing current coursework. I thought the plan sounded great; Marquel was impatient that he would not be able to play football until next season, but he did agree to the plan. Less than two weeks later, Marquel ranted obscenities at the coach and left campus.

The rants continued at teachers, students, basically anyone in the building. I soon discovered Marquel had no method of dealing with any form of disappointment, regardless of how large or small the disappointment was. After talking with his cousin, I learned his father had been incarcerated most of his life, his mother had many boyfriends in the home, and there was the possibility Marquel had fought the boyfriends to protect himself. It was evident his focus on the bad stories/memories became his identity. Marquel desperately needed a new life story.

When I talked with his teachers, one teacher shared that Marquel loved to dance. Marquel began performing at halftime for the basketball games. A male mentor was assigned to Marquel. The obscene rants were less severe and frequent, his grades improved, and Marquel started a new identity at school. The emotional struggles continued in the home. After missing a couple of days of school, his cousin stated she could no longer deal with his anger and sent him back to his mother.

A Story: Kevin

Written by Ruben Perez

Background Information

Kevin was a 10th-grade African-American male in a very diverse high school of more than 1,400 students. I was employed as a student advocate for a large school district. Shortly before Kevin's 16th birthday, his mother woke him up in the middle of the night saying that they were going to leave quietly so as not to wake up his father. Kevin felt good that they were going to finally escape the house where there had been much physical and emotional violence. He was very excited that his mother finally had the courage to leave after years of his begging her to stand up to him.

Kevin remembered the bus ride from California to Houston, Texas. It was extremely long, and he said he was hungry for most of the ride. However, all he cared about was getting away from his father. When the bus finally reached Houston, they left the bus station and walked to a nearby park. They took a seat on a bench. His mother looked at him and said, "I'll be right back." Kevin doesn't remember how long he waited, but his mother never came back. He fell asleep on the bench, and when he woke up the next morning, he realized he was now alone. He befriended a group of men on a nearby corner who were homeless. They took care of him, fed him, and somehow found a family that allowed him to stay with them for a while.

The Day I Met Kevin

The school had four assistant principals. One of them asked if I would speak to one of the students who submitted a journal entry he found both encouraging and concerning. The assignment was to write about the importance of education. Kevin had written a passionate display of wanting to go to college with a level of desperation uncommon to most students. Some of the statements in his entry were, "Without college you ain't nothing," "All these people I go to school with who can afford college don't appreciate what they got," "I barely get enough to eat and college is expensive," and, "Living on the streets is hard."

Before I met Kevin, I gathered some information about him to help me better understand how to proceed. He was known to be a quiet young man. He would easily go unnoticed. Most staff members described him as respectful and helpful. One of his teachers described him as someone who makes an effort to not be noticed.

When Kevin walked into my office, it took a while for him to conclude that I was someone to be trusted. Once he took me into his confidence, the floodgates opened immediately, and I was not prepared for what was coming. He was one week away from turning 18 when I learned he had been homeless for the last three years. I found him to be extremely intelligent and told him so. He had difficulty hearing that from me. I asked him how he had survived on the streets all this time. The following is a summary of what I was told:

> I make friends at school pretty easy. I figure out who I can ask to stay with for a week or weekend. If I make friends with their mother, I can usually stay a little longer. Most of the time they let me sleep on the sofa, but sometimes I do get a room I can share or have one to myself. I figured out that if I stay away for most of the day and come back after dark, I can usually stay longer. If I stay inside the house too long, they get nervous and I get in the way. If I don't come home until nighttime, I don't bother them as much. So sometimes I can stay at somebody's house up to four months.

> When I don't have a house to go to, I sometimes sleep in the park or under overpasses. I made some friends on the street who taught me how to keep it safe. No one in the school knows my real story because I don't want to be reported.

About a year ago I ran into my mother on the streets. When she saw me, she started crying. She never said she was sorry, but I could tell she was because the tears would not stop. She gave me a hug and asked how I was doing. I think she lives near this school because I bump into her every now and then. A couple of my friends met her. All she could say was thank you for taking care of my boy.

I continued to work with Kevin and was able to verify a lot of what he said. I located phone numbers of families he stayed with and found their stories to match his, by and large. Nobody in the community or at school had anything negative to say about Kevin. They found him to be a most remarkable young man.

Three months later he was staying with a friend who was part of an after-school club. His friend would stay after school once a week before going home. There was a strict rule that no one could be roaming the school after dismissal. Any student in the building not involved in extracurricular activities had to leave. This particular day was cold, and Kevin decided not to wait for his friend outside because he did not have a jacket. He remained in the school, hiding and trying to go unnoticed while waiting for his friend to be released. An assistant principal encountered Kevin in the hallway.

The incident was caught on video without audio. With arms pointed towards the door, the administrator requested that Kevin leave. Kevin requested he be allowed to stay and was interrupted. On the video it seems as if the discussion quickly turned into an argument. The administrator was walking towards Kevin as Kevin kept backing up. It was a very slow progression.

When Kevin's back reached the wall behind him, his anger became visible. On the video, the assistant principal's body language appears to be stern, with a finger pointing in Kevin's face. At this point, Kevin pushes the administrator hard enough that he falls backwards and slides for about three feet. As a result, the police were called, and Kevin was taken away. I got a phone call at the district office and was asked to get there before Kevin was taken into custody. I arrived minutes after the police car drove off.

After having seen the video and listening to the accounts of what happened, I decided to assist Kevin as best I could. Together with some staff members, we got a local attorney to volunteer his time and represent Kevin. I did not want his representation to come from the courts as I felt his side of the story would be easily dismissed. In the two visits I had with Kevin while he was in custody at the local jail, he continued to express a strong desire to graduate from high school. He felt the current situation was bad enough to prevent that from happening.

On the day of his hearing, the judge examined all the evidence and heard the accounts of the events. It was decided that Kevin would be dismissed with time served and placed on probation with required visits to a parole officer once a month. I asked that the parole officer visits be dismissed. The school Kevin attended was 20 miles from downtown. I explained his living conditions and the difficulty he would have getting a ride on a good day. He would most likely be late or miss an appointment, causing him to violate the terms of his probation. The judge agreed and dismissed Kevin with time served. It took approximately two days for the paperwork to be processed before his release.

Unbeknownst to me, one of his friends from school somehow got in contact with his mother. A week after Kevin's return to school, his mother appeared, asked to speak to him, and later that day checked him out of school. She had improved her living situation and acquired an apartment. Throughout the process of Kevin being checked out, he was quiet and solemn. I am hoping someday to see him again.

Reflection

I think most of us have that small circle of students we will never forget nor do we wish to forget. Kevin is just that for me. I learned a lot about myself, the school system, the justice system, and our concrete and ambiguous roles as educators. Kevin's situation put a magnifying glass on so many things that are out of our control. His living situation, his absent mother, the skills he developed simply to survive, others' perception of him and his perception of others, protective laws that expire at the age of 18, and so many of the details made any juggling act seem like child's play.

At every turn I was hit head-on with a brick wall. From one department to the next, Kevin came close to qualifying for support but fell short in one aspect or another. I was under the impression that I would be taken more seriously if I maintained objectivity and composure when I told his story. It sometimes took Herculean effort to avoid breaking down in front of somebody as I revealed intimate details of his life. I still live with questions I will never understand. How did he get registered for school? Were papers forged? How did a student's horrible situation go unnoticed for so long? What survival skills did he have to learn?

If there was one reason that Kevin opened up to me, I think it is because I believed him from start to finish. Even when I asked him for the names of the people he had stayed with in the past, I think he believed I was trying to help and not just verifying whether he was telling the truth.

As for the assistant principal, I truly believe that he was simply doing his job. When someone is an administrator at a school with more than 1,400 students, safety becomes imperative and priority one. The assistant principal had no history of being unfair. He was, however, rather stern. When he encountered Kevin in the hallway, he had less than 15 minutes to clear the halls before dismissal. After Kevin had returned to school from jail, the assistant principal expressed no complaints that I was aware of. If anything, he just remained quiet and allowed Kevin's day to go uninterrupted.

Schools would benefit greatly from discussions about their students with unique situations that cause staff members to feel paralyzed and unable to do anything. Although Kevin had support from staff members at school, all of us were caught in a whirlwind of "what ifs" and "if onlys." The paralysis was palpable.

Two Kinds of Metaphor Stories

Metaphor stories work at the subconscious level. The first kind is one in which you ask cause-and-effect questions along a narrative pattern. There are two rules: Never use the student's name, and always end on a positive note.

An Example: Derek and the Substitute Teacher

When I was a principal, I had a fifth-grade student who did extremely well in school except when there was a substitute. Then I would see him in my office within 10–20 minutes of school starting. And unfortunately, he had a teacher who was frequently sick. I realized that the only times I saw him were over this substitute issue, so I called him into my office. We'll call the student Derek (remember, never use their real names).

I said to him, "Will you help me tell a story?"

Derek said, "Is that story about me?"

I said, "It can be if you want it to be, but I am not in the fifth grade, and there are things that I don't know about being a fifth-grader."

He said, "Okay."

I said, "Once upon a time there was a boy. This boy was very smart and got along great in school—except when a substitute came to teach the boy's class. What did the boy do when there was a substitute?"

He said, "He threw paper, made jokes, and caused trouble." (Which was exactly what Derek was doing.)

I said, "What do the boy's friends think about that?" (I wanted to know if his motivation was peer support.)

He said, "They are confused. They do not know what to think." (This answer let me know he was not doing it for his friends.)

I said, "What does the boy do when the regular teacher is teaching the class?"

He said, "He sits in his seat and takes notes and pays attention."

I said, "Why doesn't the boy do that with a substitute teacher?"

He said, "I don't know."

I thought there might be a reason he wanted to come to the office. I said to him, "What happens to the boy when he throws paper, makes jokes, and causes trouble?"

He said, "He gets sent to the office."

I said, "What happens to him when he gets to the office?"

He said, "The principal says it can't happen again." (Yeah, like that really worked!)

Knowing that students bring behaviors into school from outside school, I said to him, "What does the boy do at home?"

He said, "Depends which house he is in." (His mom and dad are divorced. He has learned very young to change out behaviors depending on who is in charge. I was thinking he would use one set of behaviors because school is always the same place. That is a foreign idea for him, since his behavior is dependent upon who is in charge.)

At this point you want to build a solution into the story. I said to him, "What the boy needs to do is use one set of behaviors all the time, regardless of who is in charge, because school is always the same place. Can the boy do that?"

He said, "Yes."

I said, "What are the behaviors it's okay to use in school?"

He told me.

I finished the story this way: "So the boy started using one set of behaviors all the time. He used the set he used with the regular teacher, regardless of who was in charge, because the classroom was always the same place. The boy was very successful, and his friends knew what to expect."

I did not see him again for any discipline reason.

The second kind of metaphor story is one in which you simply tell a story. Here are examples of different stories you can tell for different reasons. Aesop's fables are metaphor stories. A metaphor story goes beneath the conscious mind and impacts thinking. Didactic stories are a kind of metaphor story and carry instructions about behavior and thinking to the subconscious.

The Dog and the Shadow

It happened that a dog had got a piece of meat and was carrying it home in his mouth to eat it in peace. Now, on his way home he had to cross a plank lying across a running brook. As he crossed, he looked down and saw his own shadow reflected in the water beneath. Thinking it was another dog with another piece of meat, he made up his mind to have that also. So he made a snap at the shadow in the water, but as he opened his mouth, the piece of meat fell out, dropped into the water, and was never seen more.

Beware lest you lose the substance by grasping at the shadow.

The Wolf and the Crane

A wolf had been gorging on an animal he had killed when suddenly a small bone in the meat stuck in his throat and he could not swallow it. He soon felt terrible pain in his throat and ran up and down groaning and groaning and seeking for something to relieve the pain. He tried to induce everyone he met to remove the bone. "I would give anything," said he, "if you would take it out." At last the crane agreed to try, and told the wolf to lie on his side and open his jaws as wide as he could. Then the crane put its long neck down the wolf's throat, and with its beak loosened the bone, till at last it got it out. "Will you kindly give me the reward you promised?" said the Crane. The wolf grinned and showed his teeth and said: "Be content. You have put your head inside a wolf's mouth and taken it out again in safety; that ought to be reward enough for you."

Gratitude and greed go not together.

Here is a rewritten Aesop fable for porn addiction.

The Boy Who Loved Porn

(Rewrite of "Avaricious and Envious")

There was a teenage boy who loved porn. Watching porn was easier than talking to girls. He could masturbate, find more and more exciting porn, and watch two or three porn clips at once. He loved it. He did it many times a week, and when his anxieties would increase, he did it more. When he got into high school, he tried sex "in person" and did not like it. He found it difficult to get an erection. He even tried some of the activities he had seen in porn clips—he slapped his partner and choked her, but she did not like it. He went back to porn, but in his mid-20s he stopped being able to get an erection at all. He tried giving up porn for a while in an effort to "reboot," but that took too long. He could not give up masturbation and porn, but masturbation and porn did not work anymore, and he became more anxious than ever. His life as he knew it no longer worked.

Vice has its own punishments.

Another Example: The Queen and the Princess

When I was a principal, we had a sixth-grade girl who was brilliant (with an IQ of more than 140) but who was not doing her work. She had a stunningly beautiful mother. The girl was very pretty, but her mother was stunning. We told the girl this story, and the next day she started working.

Once upon a time there was a very pretty princess who had a stunningly beautiful mother, the queen. The queen wore big robes that went way out from her body and gave her a presence as well as making her more beautiful. Often the princess would stand so close to her mother, the queen, that she would get caught up in the robes and no one could see her. However, the princess was very smart and also very pretty. She knew that she had her own abilities, talents, and beauty. She decided to stand far enough away from the queen so that she did not get caught in her robes. Then she could be seen for her own abilities, talents, and beauty without dishonoring the queen. And she did that. She was recognized for her own talents, beauty, and abilities.

> **The following books give many, many examples of metaphor stories that can be used with kids or teens:**
>
> *101 Healing Stories for Kids and Teens: Using Metaphors in Therapy* by George W. Burns
>
> *The Big Book of ACT Metaphors: A Practitioner's Guide to Experiential Exercises and Metaphors in Acceptance and Commitment Therapy* by Jill Stoddard and Niloofar Afari
>
> *Handbook of Therapeutic Storytelling* by Stefan Hammel

All metaphor stories, to be successful, must represent the problem in some fashion, identify a process or "how to" to go about solving the problem, and then end with the problem resolved—a solution.

The following is a metaphor story from Hammel's book. This story is for addiction, depression, habit, motivation, and neglect and shows how an attitude of resignation can turn a minor issue into a disaster.

The Cart, the Mud, and I

When I forgot to steer the cart around the mud, I said to myself, "It's too late to do anything now," and I waited to see what would happen.

When I pushed the cart right into the mud, I said to myself, "It's too late to do anything now," and I waited to see what would happen.

When the cart sank in the mud and I sank along with it, I said to myself, "It's too late to do anything now," and I waited to see what would happen.

When the cart disappeared in the mud, and I disappeared along with it, I knew what I had always known.[105]

When I tell this story, I wait for a moment after the end of the story. Then I finish the story this way:

As the cart and I were sinking, I remembered a movie in which a person and a cart were sinking in the mud. As the mud got to my throat, I threw up my arm and yelled for help. A person walking down the road threw me a rope, which I caught, and I struggled and allowed the person with the rope to slowly pull me out. I said to myself, "It's never too late to do something."

The following quotation from Rebecca Solnit can also help debrief the story:

> Most of us don't change until we have to, and crisis is often what obliges us to do so. Crises are often resolved only through a new identity and new purpose, whether it's that of a nation or a single human being.[106]

Betrayals

Many wounds come in the form of a betrayal.

It is important to remember that betrayals are never about you. They are about the person who did them and that person's driving emotional force to address an injury/need that they have.

Examples of betrayals are legendary in literature, in religion, in history. They are part of the human condition. From Shakespeare's portrayal of betrayal in Julius Ceasar (*Et tu, Brute?*), to the betrayal of Jesus by Judas for 30 pieces of silver, to the betrayal of the German people by Hitler, almost all betrayals are about the person doing the betraying. But in the limbic system, a betrayal is portrayed as "there is something wrong with me."

One of the most intense betrayals is death. It is such a loss. And if loss of a parent occurs for an adolescent—particularly between the ages of 12 and 15—the emotional intensity is life-altering.

Strategy: Swapping a Toxic Coauthor with a Healthy Coauthor

Key parts of anyone's stories are who they identify as "coauthors." Coauthors can be toxic or healthy, but either way, they help you write the story of who you are. Coauthors are individuals who are in our lives and who help us shape the stories of ourselves.[107]

There is a technique you can use with a student when they tell you that they can't do something. In this technique, you have an individual recall an incident that was negative. You ask them who was present when that happened. What were the comments that were made? Then you ask them for the name of someone who was very supportive to them. Ask them to switch out the "negative" coauthor with the "positive, supportive" coauthor. Then you replay the scenario with the comments from the positive coauthor.

I have a friend who had a very negative parent. This parent constantly berated him, particularly in middle and high school. I asked him if he had had an adult in high school who liked him. He said yes, so I asked him to replay the scenario with the positive adult rather than the negative one. What would the positive person say? He was amazed. Basically, this exercise can allow the negative memory to be significantly reduced. It helps a person understand that any situation can be played out several different ways depending on the coauthor who is present.

"The present rearranges the past. We never tell the story whole because a life isn't a story; it's a Milky Way of events, and we are forever picking out constellations from it to fit who and where we are."[108]

Chapter Summary

1. The hippocampus carries the story of who you are.

2. Developing a story of who you are is a very important task. It is constructed through a narrative, and it is constructed with those around you.

3. Keeping a story coherent over time and over contexts is critical in maintaining your well-being.

4. All lives involve wounds. If you allow the wounds to define you, your growth stagnates. If you allow your wounds to become a part of you, your growth will continue. It is the difference between having a gaping, unhealed cut and having a scar.

5. Metaphor stories are a way of changing behavior because they impact the subconscious.

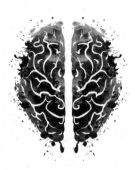

5 When the Adults Are Stressed

Strategies for secondary traumatic stress or compassion fatigue in adults

Why is this important? When a person is stressed and in a high state of emotional arousal, information processing suffers tremendously. When the adults are stressed, the ability to teach is significantly reduced, as is the ability to respond with appropriate actions.

Stress Is a Lot Like an Iceberg

A person is only able to identify about 10% of what their issues are in the cortex, or conscious mind. About 90% of stress is held in the cellular memory in every cell and in the brain, in the subconscious and unconscious. The hypothalamic-pituitary-adrenal (HPA) axis of the body regulates our stress. When we are in chronic stress—daily—the HPA axis stays on, and the long-lasting effects impact our physical, emotional, and psychological wellness. It is not the stress itself that is the problem but the body's response to the stress, which is called allostatic load. Managing this stress

wears the body down. Stress overloads the prefrontal cortex, which makes it harder to regulate emotions and thoughts.[109]

Over the years, if there is a great deal of stress, the body's allostatic load remains high.

How Do You Know You Are Stressed?

Stress shows up in your HRV—your heart rate variability number.

If you have a Fitbit or an Apple Watch, just go to the heart icon, and it will provide your individual HRV. HRV is a measure of your autonomic nervous system (ANS). The following charts of normative HRV scored by age and gender are provided by Elite HRV.[110]

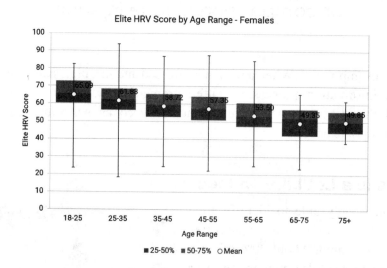

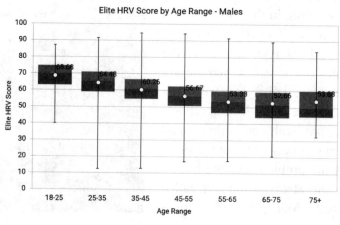

High is good; low is poor. A high HRV is associated with healthiness. A low HRV is associated with illness. A high HRV indicates the body has an adaptive quality for the maintenance of a healthy body.

HRV measures the balance or lack of balance in the system.

The Autonomic Nervous System

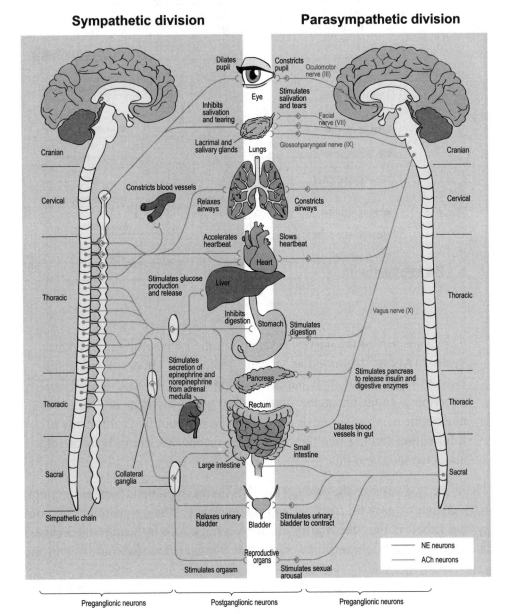

Sympathetic division   **Parasympathetic division**

Parasympathetic Nervous System (PNS) and Sympathetic Nervous System (SNS)

The following chart is from the HeartMath Institute.[111]

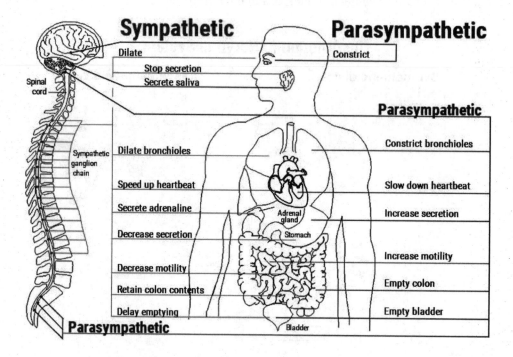

The larger part of the nervous system is called the autonomic nervous system (ANS). "Autonomic" means "automatic" because we don't have to think about it. It happens automatically. In fact, 99.99% of everything going on in the body at any given moment is under the autonomic nervous system's control. We have about five trillion bits of information coming into the brain every second. We are only aware of about ten thousand bits.[112]

There are two parts to the ANS: The PNS (parasympathetic nervous system) is in charge of growth, healing, and maintenance. The sympathetic nervous system (SNS) is the "fire alarm." It plays a huge role in health and sickness and is part of the "fight or flight" system. It is intended to save our lives in any given crisis.

When we go into fight or flight, many things happen. Blood flow completely changes. It's no longer going to the stomach to digest food. It's no longer going to the frontal lobes of the brain...or the kidneys and liver. The lion's share of the blood is now going to the muscles because your body thinks that it is going to have to fight harder or run faster than whatever is threatening your life. So you don't need to digest that food in the bowel or clear the toxins from the liver, balance the electrolytes in the kidneys, or have creative thought because if you don't survive the next few minutes, all of that doesn't matter. Again, these things happen automatically.[113]

When the SNS goes off, our cells cease their normal growth, healing, and maintenance. Alexander Loyd cites research from Stanford: "Our cells do not get nutrition, oxygen, minerals...[They] do not get rid of waste products and toxins while under stress. Everything stops except what is necessary to survive. This results in an environment inside of the cell that is toxic and does not allow for growth and repair."[114]

On the flip side, the same research at Stanford found that cells that are open and in the growth and healing mode are literally impervious to illness and disease.

The SNS—The Fire Alarm

When the SNS goes off (when the fire alarm sounds), "a direct message goes out from the brain to the immune system through cells that are directly connected to the end of nerves. They are called dendrites."[115] Dendrites give off nerve transmitters and are called "neural immune cells." They are a direct link to the immune system. Their message is to stop and shut down.

The SNS is about survival, so everything gets shut down that is not crucial to survival. That includes the immune system. The immune system uses a huge amount of energy.

When the fire alarm goes off, it is about survival.

- Blood flow in your body completely changes. Blood leaves your digestive system; it no longer goes to the prefrontal cortex, kidneys, or liver. Blood goes to the muscles.

- Cells cease their normal growth, healing, and maintenance.

- Cells do not get nutrition, oxygen, or minerals. Waste is not removed from the cells. The environment inside the cells becomes toxic. Cells cannot repair themselves.

- Immune system shuts down.

Stress is controlled in the central nervous system. As stated previously, physiological stress is created and regulated through the hypothalamic-pituitary-adrenal (HPA) axis. The HPA axis serves as a central processing unit for the whole brain. It has connections to the limbic system—the emotional centers of the brain. It also has nerve connections to every part of the brain and all of your body through the hormones it manufactures and releases through the pituitary gland. The pituitary gland releases hormones into the blood.

The hypothalamus controls blood pressure, body temperature, regulation of body water by thirst and kidney function, uterine contractility, breast milk, emotional drives, growth hormone, adrenal glands, thyroid hormone, and sex organ function.

Heart rate variability testing measures the increase and decrease of the heart rate in relation to breathing patterns. It tells you the balance in the autonomic nervous system. "The balance of the ANS equals growth and healing, which adds up to health, whereas imbalance or stress in the system leads to disease and ill health."[116]

How does the body manifest stress? Through the weakest link. It could be a genetic predisposition, the result of a toxin we have ingested, or from a prior physical injury.

Physical Issues Related to the ANS Being Out of Balance

Autonomic function imbalances are associated with:

- Depression
- Hypoglycemia
- Panic disorder
- Sleep disorder
- Asthma
- Fatigue
- Dizziness
- Nausea
- Irritable bowel syndrome
- Fibromyalgia
- Hypertension
- Chemical sensitivity
- Premenstrual syndrome
- Anxiety
- Migraine
- Arrhythmia[117]

Stress is caused by insufficient energy. The fire alarm goes off. The cells shut down to conserve energy in the body, oxygen isn't getting into the cells, nutrients aren't getting into the cells, and glucose (fuel for the cells) isn't getting into the cells. The power plants of the cell are being starved. As mentioned previously, these little power plants are called mitochondria. Mitochondria look like bacteria.

A cell has to have oxygen and glucose and be able to exhaust the waste out of the cell. When you stop that process, you get a "brownout" and then a "blackout," and eventually the cell dies. This causes an energy shortage, which leads to cellular damage—which we call disease.

Cells can function if the mitochondria stay alive.

"A healing code changes destructive energy frequencies and signals into healthy frequencies and signals."[118]

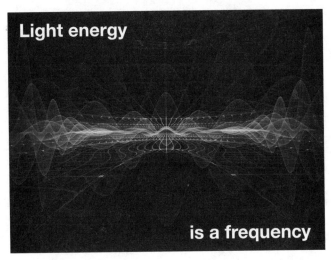

Light energy

is a frequency

The way you change the frequency is to hit it with one that is exactly the opposite.

You can stop the hypothalamus from sending the energy frequency signal that initiates a stress signal.

How? By using energy.

Transfer of information through chemicals and nutritionals is about one centimeter per second. Transfer of information through energy occurs at around 186,000 miles per second.

The healing code stops the hypothalamus from sending the energy frequency signal that initiates a stress response.[119]

The first things stress turns off are the healing and immune systems, and when the healing and immune systems are turned back on and turned way up, they are capable of healing just about anything.

The HeartMath Institute's research indicates that activation of certain memories appears to damage DNA, while activation of healthy memories may heal DNA.[120]

Stress in the parents created destructive cellular memories that ended up manifesting as stress in the children.[121]

We looked at the following graphics from the HeartMath Institute earlier in the book, but they are worth reinvestigating in light of what we now know about HRV, stress, and healing codes.

Frequencies from the Heart—Love[122]

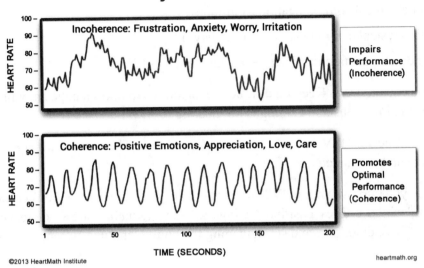

Heart-Rhythm Patterns

Incoherence: Frustration, Anxiety, Worry, Irritation

Impairs Performance (Incoherence)

Coherence: Positive Emotions, Appreciation, Love, Care

Promotes Optimal Performance (Coherence)

TIME (SECONDS)

©2013 HeartMath Institute

heartmath.org

A Boy and His Dog[123]

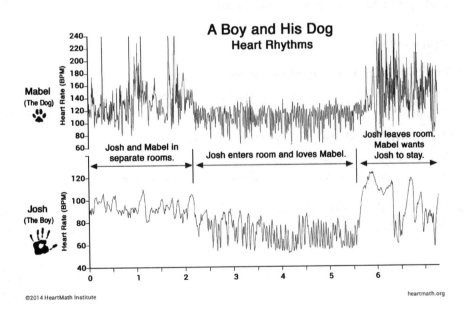

A Boy and His Dog
Heart Rhythms

Mabel (The Dog)

Josh (The Boy)

Josh and Mabel in separate rooms.

Josh enters room and loves Mabel.

Josh leaves room. Mabel wants Josh to stay.

©2014 HeartMath Institute

heartmath.org

The Heart and Its Communications

The heart communicates with the brain and body in four ways:

- Neurological communication (nervous system)
- Biochemical communication (hormones)
- Biophysical communication (pulse wave)
- Energetic communication (electromagnetic fields)[124]

Coping equals stress. Keeping destructive memories requires a huge amount of energy, and it's constant. Coping is not healing.

The good news: HRV is not a permanent condition. The autonomic nervous system can be changed.

How do you improve your HRV? You can activate your parasympathetic nervous system, which creates positive feelings, thereby reducing stress, increasing your positive emotions, and strengthening the body's immune system.[125]

Getting into Coherence

Definitions of coherence:

- **Clarity of thought, speech, and emotional composure**
  *The quality of being orderly, consistent, and intelligible
  (e.g., a coherent sentence)*

- **Synchronization or entrainment between multiple waveforms**
  *A constructive waveform produced by two or more waves that
  are phase- or frequency-locked*

- **Order within a singular oscillatory waveform**
  *An ordered or constructive distribution of power content
  within a single waveform; autocoherence (e.g., sine wave)*[126]

The following discussion of noise cancellation is reprinted with permission from Ron Kurtus's School for Champions.[127]

Simple Wave Cancellation

Although sound is a compression wave, each tone or frequency can be represented by a sine wave of a given wavelength.

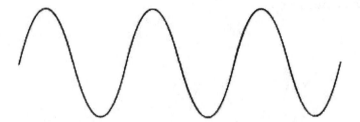

Simple sine wave for single sound frequency

Slightly Out of Phase

Suppose another pure sound of the same frequency was emitted, but just a fraction of a second later. That means it is slightly out of phase from the first sound or sine wave. The visual representation of the two waves would be as in the next illustration.

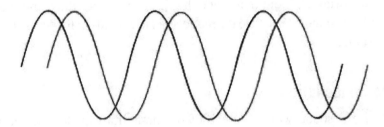

One pure sound a fraction of a second after the next

Graphing the Result

You can graphically see what the resulting wave would look like by adding values above and below the centerline (zero). This is illustrated by the dots in the following drawing. The line with all the dots is approximately a sine wave of the same frequency.

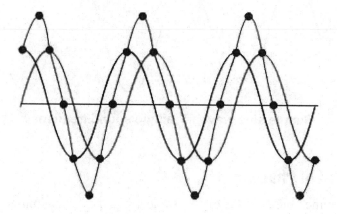

Sum of two waves slightly out of phase

You would hear the same frequency, except that the sound would be twice as loud as the original. Note that since the frequencies are the same, you would not hear beat sounds. (See "Beat Frequencies in Sound"[128] for more information on that subject.)

Sound Cancellation

Finally, if the sound waves were 180° or one-half a wavelength out of phase, the sum of the waveforms would be zero. They would cancel out each other and there would be no sound.

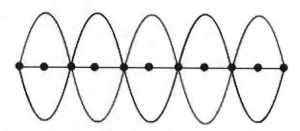

Sum of waves equals zero sound

How to Do Cancellation of Your Subconscious Memories

There is a method to cancel out subconscious memories noninvasively. Subconscious memories are stored cellularly. This method was developed by Alexander Loyd in his book, *The Healing Code.* It takes six minutes twice a day.

One of my consultants who grew up in extreme poverty is now in her late 60s. Because she was often hungry as a young child, she always carries food with her after a meal. In fact, among foster children, it is very common that they will hide food in their room so that they have it in case they need it. Using Loyd's technique, my consultant was able to end that practice.

According to Loyd,

> You activate the healing centers with your fingers…The hands and fingers direct flows of energy at the healing centers. The healing centers activate an energetic healing system that functions in a manner parallel to the immune system. Instead of killing viruses and bacteria, it targets memories related to the issue the person is thinking about. Using positive, healing energy frequencies, it cancels out and replaces the negative, destructive frequencies.[129]

If you are interested in learning more about this technique, please get a copy of Alexander Loyd's book.

How Mirror Neurons Impact Compassion[130]

One of the reasons we can feel compassion is that our brain has mirror neurons. This is one of the reasons that emotions are contagious.

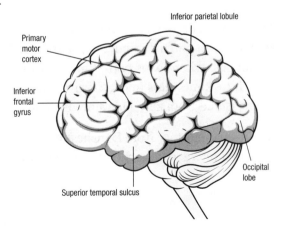

Mirror Neuron System

Inferior parietal lobule

Primary motor cortex

Inferior frontal gyrus

Occipital lobe

Superior temporal sulcus

"[The] mirror neuron system is a group of specialized neurons that 'mirrors' the actions and behavior of others. The involvement of [the] mirror neuron system (MNS) is implicated in neurocognitive functions (social cognition, language, empathy, theory of mind) and neuropsychiatric disorders."[131]

The Role of Epigenetics, Historical Trauma, and Intergenerational Trauma

Stress can be carried intergenerationally. During the 9-11 terror attacks, there were 200 women in the immediate vicinity who were pregnant. When the babies were born, they were all tested. If the mother was in the first or second trimester of pregnancy, the babies were "normal." But if the mother was in the last trimester of pregnancy, every one of the babies was born with a permanently elevated level of cortisol.

What is epigenetics? Only about 10% of your DNA is actually defined genetically. Your DNA has genetic predispositions that the environment can switch "on" or "off."

If there has been generational trauma (slavery, war, abuse), then that can be passed on genetically. Additionally, it is always passed on in the stories that are told. Usually the trauma is passed on genetically to the child of the person who experiences the trauma if it is going to be passed through genetically. In some of the research, it was determined that if the trauma happened to the person while the female was in vitro (when the eggs are made), then it could change the DNA in the eggs. If the trauma happened to the male when he was going through puberty and making sperm, then it showed up in the offspring of that male.

One of the adults who participated in Getting Ahead, which is our program to work with parents in poverty, said this: "You know, my mother was a meth addict, and when I was born, I had a meth addiction. I started out at a minus 3 or 4. It took me years to get to zero." He went on to say that growth should not be measured from zero but rather from where the person started.

The following story from Dr. Chestin Auzenne-Curl is an example of stress that is passed intergenerationally through stories.

Arthur Chenier (1877–1946)

Written by Chestin Auzenne-Curl

I wrote the following as a Facebook post after the July 6 murder of Philando Castile in 2016. Many of my friends on both ends of the political spectrum were struggling to understand how the tragedy could have occurred. There were discussions that positioned advocates for the redress of police brutality in opposition to supporters of police. It was a stream of Black vs. "blue" lives mattering. I recognized it as communal pain and for many, a reckoning of cognitive dissonance, so I shared a story of my mother's grandfather who was both Black (by birth) and blue (by choice):

> This is Arthur Chenier, one of my mother's grandfathers. He came to Texas from Opelousas, Louisiana, to be a sheriff in the Southeast Houston area. The area was ill-prepared for a Black sheriff at a time when Blacks were not allowed to be seen in public with firearms. He was the first.
>
> He was also shot and killed in Baytown, Texas, shortly after taking the job.
>
> When his son traveled to Texas to claim the body, he met a BEAUTIFUL, young, widowed SUPERWOMAN with two young children, and the two wed shortly after they met. My mother is the youngest of their five children together.
>
> I argue the nation is still not quite ready for Black men and open carry…the image was illegal just two generations ago. The evidence is in this photo. You will notice scratch marks across his left hand—at the hip area. He was told that it didn't matter that he was sheriff. He wasn't above the law and couldn't be photographed with a weapon. So the picture was defaced before his assassination.

This post created space for a less-tense discussion centered on just how many members of the Black community had similar stories. Several shared oral histories of family members murdered or brutalized by officers. Still, the promise of enacting change has remained. Black Americans devote themselves to serving and protecting a public in which they feel neither served nor protected. My great-grandfather's murder brought my family back to the Second Amendment in a heavy spirit that reminded us that when all men were guaranteed this right, Black men were not counted as men. Coincidentally, my great-grandfather's death certificate was "misplaced," and the area's census records omit his promotion from janitor to officer.

What Is Secondary Traumatic Stress or Compassion Fatigue?

I worked with an elementary school in Lake County, Illinois. This was a high-poverty school. Approximately 35% of the students had at least one incarcerated parent. On top of that, the school district had put the medically fragile special education unit in that building. A student in that unit could die at any time. Teachers were packing lunches for students to take home because the students were hungry. The level of compassion fatigue and secondary traumatic stress was high. The principal called me and said, "Is there anything we can do? The burnout is so high. Teachers are in tears."

I met with the teachers for five staff meetings, and we did the following: We went through the five stages of grief outlined by Elizabeth Kübler-Ross, identified the greatest stressors, looked at the research of Stephen Covey on the circle of influence versus the circle of concern, and then we put together a plan based on what we could do. The teachers contacted local churches and established a food pantry at school. The churches were told specifically what to donate—canned or pouched tuna and other meats, beans, and crackers. The goal was to have food that (a) could be carried in a backpack, (b) could be eaten even if there was no electricity or the appliances did not work, and (c) was high in protein. Food in poverty is high in carbohydrates and fat but not in protein. It takes much longer for the body to metabolize protein as opposed to carbohydrates, so with high-protein foods, the body has nutrients longer. The focus then moved to what we could do as a group.

What Is Compassion Fatigue?

Compassion fatigue refers to the profound emotional and physical exhaustion that helping professionals and caregivers can develop over the course of their career as helpers. It is a gradual erosion of all the things that keep us connected to others in our caregiver role: our empathy, our hope, and of course, our compassion—not only for others, but also for ourselves.[132]

Compassion fatigue has these symptoms: unhappy at work, bitter at life, help create a toxic work environment, irritated, prone to judgment, ignore professional boundaries, and become callous toward students and parents.

What Is Secondary Traumatic Stress?

I have never cried as much for a student as I did when I was an elementary principal and had a kindergarten student who was being sexually abused. He had already started to disassociate parts of his body—he would tell me that his "hand was bad." He acted out in the playhouse sexual activities (and described how they felt) in ways that one can only know through personal experience. His mother was mentally ill and had a drug addiction. The one time she came to see me, she was so drugged that she could barely function. The child had been adopted by the mother and her former husband. She had divorced, and then she married the man who was the abuser. I called child protective services, but nothing happened. I called the state police because there was no birth certificate and was told that the boy was just having fantasies—that a 5-year-old did not know what was happening. For several nights I would go home and cry. The boy would come to school with his eyes in so much pain he could barely focus. He started subjecting fellow students to the treatment he was receiving.

To this day, that situation haunts me. I wonder what happened to the boy. I do know that I did everything I could. But it was not enough.

The pain I experienced in dealing with the situation—my feelings of helplessness, frustration, and crying—that is secondary traumatic stress.

Reporting Child Abuse

One of the places where educator stress may be high is in the legal requirement to report child abuse. Particularly at the secondary level, the relationship with the student may be broken. Adding to the stress is the knowledge that many times nothing positive happens for the child as the result of the reporting. Sometimes the situation for the student is even worse. When I taught secondary school, I was always upfront with the students. I told them: "Before you tell me this, please know that by law, I must report any abuse that occurs. I am not betraying you. It is a legal requirement."

Ten Signs That You Are Emotionally Exhausted

Here are 10 signs of emotional exhaustion…

- Fear creeps into your life.
- You find yourself running away from things.
- You back out of relationships.
- You make foolish decisions impulsively.
- You push yourself past your physical limits.
- Your work seems pointless.
- You complain that you want to quit and give up.
- You feel isolated and attacked.
- You compare yourself to others and feel bad about yourself.
- You think death might bring relief.[133]

Indicators of Where You Are on the ANS Continuum[134]

	Apathetic/depressed	Safe, clear thinking, ready to act
States of being	Depressed, doesn't care	Safe, clear, alert
Arousal of ANS	Too low	Low to moderate
Muscles	Loose, slack	Relaxed, toned
Breathing	From the upper chest	Easy, from the abdomen
Heartbeat	Slow	Resting
Pupils, eyes, eyelids	Lids lower, smaller pupils	Eyelids relaxed, pupils normal
Temperature of hands	Warm or cool	Warm
Likely feelings	Grief, shame, unhappy	Calm, love, excitement, pleasure
Contact with self and others	Withdrawn	Accessible, likes contact
Prefrontal cortex	Depends on whether it is accessible or not	Accessible

Reactive, senses danger	Getting ready to escape
Reactive, wants to run or fight	Wants to freeze
High	Overload
Tense	Rigid
Fast, often upper chest	Hyperventilates
Quick/forceful	Very fast
Eyelids tense, pupils dilated	Eyelids very tense, pupils small or dilated
Cold	Extremes of cold and hot
Feelings stop	May evacuate bowel or bladder
Limited	Not likely
Limited access	Access probably not possible

Stress Generally Comes in These Areas

The Vagus Nerve

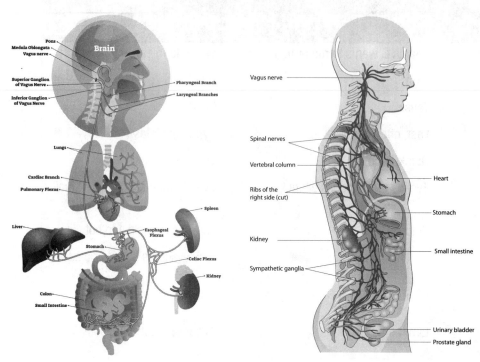

In the book *The Success Codes: Unlocking the Cellular Secrets of Success,* Alexander Loyd says, "Dr. Bruce Lipton talks about how any given cell in the body at any given moment is in one of two modes. It is either in growth mode or self-protection mode. Self-protection mode is the shut-down state of a cell that is in fight-or-flight mode."[135]

The vagus nerve is the longest nerve in the ANS.

What does your vagus nerve do? It connects the brain stem to the body.

It interfaces with the parasympathetic nervous system.

Tools for Balancing: Vagus Nerve Exercises to Restore Social Engagement

- Basic exercise
- Half-salamander exercise
- Twist and turn exercise for the trapezius[136]

Basic Exercise

- Lie on your back.

- Weave the fingers of your two hands together.

- Put your woven fingers on the back of your head.

- Keep your head in place. Using only your eyes, move your eyes to the right as far as you can. After about 30–60 seconds, you will either swallow, yawn, or sigh. This is a sign that your ANS is relaxing.

- Bring your eyes back to the center.

- Repeat eye movement as far as you can to the left.

- Sit up.

Half-Salamander Exercise

- Sit or stand comfortably.

- Face forward. Tilt your head to the right so that your right ear moves closer to your right shoulder without lifting the shoulder to meet it.

- Hold this position for 30–60 seconds.

- Let your head come back up to neutral.

- Do the same toward the left side.

Twist and Turn Exercise for the Trapezius

- Fold your arms across your chest with each hand on the opposite elbow.

- Rotate your folded arms back and forth across your chest at the level of your waist. Do so for 30–60 seconds or until you swallow, sigh, or yawn.

- Repeat the rotation at the level of your breasts.

- Repeat the rotation at the highest level you can do—at face level if possible.

Sources of Stress: Which Ones Are True for You?

Source of stress	Highlight those which apply. Go back over your highlighted list and identify the top five.
Expectations	Work Demands by self to self Family Friends Household
Relationships	Marital/partnership Children Parents Colleagues Boss Siblings/in-laws Friends Exes
Time demands	Work Household Exercise Social
Physical	Death Addiction Illness/disease Aging Exercise
Financial	Debt Insufficient income Retirement savings Too many bills Divorce payments/child support
Past memories/ wounds	

Assessing Current Level of Stress

Green Light

1. Got enough sleep last night.
2. Had food—particularly protein.
3. My children and/or partner/spouse are good.
4. I am getting exercise.
5. Have a plan for the day.
6. Traffic was sane.
7. Plenty of water—hydrated.

Yellow Light

1. Got sleep but not as much as I need.
2. Skipped breakfast/lunch.
3. Argument this morning before work.
4. Stupid memo came from the administration.
5. Johnny threw a chair the first hour of school—plan for the day is off.
6. Not enough water.
7. Who has time to go to the bathroom?

Red Light

1. Disrupted sleep, not nearly enough.
2. No exercise for four days.
3. Can't get my own child's issues diagnosed accurately.
4. Angry parent called this morning.
5. Personal financial budget is stressed.
6. Mostly sugar and carbs for food.
7. Seriously dehydrated.

Chapter Summary

1. To reduce stress, identify whether you are at a green, yellow, or red light. What can you change?

2. Stress often comes from expectations. What are your expectations?

3. What is your HRV?

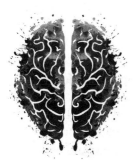

A Brain-Based Approach to Parents/Caregivers: The Emotional Dance of Parenting

There are few things in life more stressful or emotional than parenting

"Parents are not just any old people. Parents are the first people with whom we form relationships, the first people with whom we begin to appreciate the overlap and distinction between self and other. They are active agents in their children's identity development...They are also among the first people who tell us stories. They are people with a special role to play as co-habitants and co-creators of their children's narrative ecology."[137]

A Story: Celeste

Written by Norma Vijeila, principal of an alternative school in California

Celeste was being raised by a single mother and since birth had been living in her grandmother's home. Celeste had attended several high schools in South Los Angeles, and at 17 years old was enrolled at ours. Many students at our school knew or had heard of Celeste before she arrived. Celeste made her presence known at our school within the first week of school.

The first time I met Celeste, it was because she had reported that a female teacher was harassing her. Celeste told a male teacher of social studies that the female teacher of English had been spreading rumors about her. The male teacher did not feel comfortable dealing with the situation and requested that I offer a meeting to find out more about Celeste's concerns. On that same day, because many at the school heard about Celeste's concerns, I cleared my schedule to meet with her.

Celeste was a girl who spoke loud and fast and gave the most details about any situation. She told her stories in circles, and sometimes she landed on an idea or a detail about her complaint. She had to be reminded to watch her language more than a handful of times. She had a vibrant personality that took over any room she was in. During our conversation, I found out that she had felt harassed by the English teacher because she had been asked to not sit in the teacher's chair. She stated that the female teacher had used common bad words in the process of asking her—multiple times—to get off her chair. After being asked to get off the chair, Celeste stormed out of the classroom and began cursing loudly in the hallway. Celeste was a new student at our school, but in just a few days of attendance, she had made her presence heard and seen.

While Celeste was in my office, I dialed her mom's cell phone number. It went straight to voicemail, and the voicemail was full. I told Celeste I would meet with her and her mom the next day. Celeste warned me that her mom would not be happy about how she was being treated at the new school. I tried calling her mom again in the evening but was not able to make contact with her.

The next morning as I arrived at the school, I was notified that an "angry parent" was waiting for me. Celeste and her mom had arrived at school early to talk to me about their concerns. Celeste's mom was extremely agitated. She had heard the story very differently than the way we had heard it. She also claimed that the school administration had failed to call a parent since her daughter was a minor and claiming harassment. It took about 45 minutes to calm Celeste's mom down. She and Celeste circled around the veracity of what had actually happened. As it turned out, the teacher had asked Celeste to stop using her chair. The teacher did not want any students sitting in her space. At the end of the meeting, Celeste's mom called Celeste a liar since she had not provided any evidence of harassment. Celeste's mom had transitioned from yelling at me to yelling at her daughter, then she finally calmed down and thanked me for taking the time to clear up this situation.

This was only the first meeting with this student and her parent. Celeste continually exhibited the same behavior as her mother. She could go from calm and composed to angry and boisterous in a matter of seconds. She had various episodes where she would explode in anger and proceed to threaten teachers and students. Security and administrators were constantly called to remove Celeste from the classroom. Every time there was an episode, we would call her mom. Celeste would always remind us that if her mom were to come to the school, we would have to deal with her anger. Her mom's anger was one that also filled a room.

Before meeting with Celeste and her mom, I always had to remind myself that all behavior is communication, and we would have to figure out how to support Celeste to change her behavior. I also had to remind myself that our first value at my school was to care for our students and their parents. It was tough to try to change Celeste's behavior when her behavior mirrored her mom's behavior, and at times Celeste was better-behaved than her mom. The second meeting with her mom was a complete surprise. During this meeting she decided she would not make any type of contact with me. She sat in the chair next to me at the table, and Celeste sat next to her. Celeste's mom was behaving like a 4-year-old throwing a tantrum: hands crossed, lips pursed, looking down angrily. When I started the meeting, Celeste's mom took out her cell phone and started to play a video game. She then turned her chair so her back was facing me and told me to talk to her back. She said she did not want to look at me. I was shocked to see Celeste's mom modeling such behavior for her daughter. I continued to address the concern, but we did not agree, and this time Celeste's mom did not express her concerns loudly. Instead, she stormed out of the office.

We never suspended Celeste; rather, the teachers, counselors, psychologist, and the administration team collaborated to work towards recognizing the triggers to her behavior. Over two years we continued to have multiple episodes where Celeste's mom had to attend meetings to address Celeste's behavior. Her mom's behavior, similar to Celeste's, was unpredictable. The most important lesson I learned about intervening in parents' problematic behavior is that the only behavior I can control is my own. I learned how to calm myself and change my energy with the intention of changing Celeste's mom's energy. It sometimes worked.

The very last meeting with Celeste's mom occurred after I sent a letter to their home to request a formal meeting. Celeste's behavior had escalated to the point that teachers and students had been threatened, and her actions were now grounds for suspension or expulsion. Celeste's mom came to school the day after she received the letter. She went into the reception office as soon as the school opened to notify the front-office staff that she would be waiting for me in the parking lot. She was angry and used many colorful words to describe me. She said she would be sitting in her car until I arrived. My front-office staff called me immediately and notified security of the potential threat. Minutes later, I arrived at school and saw Celeste and her mom sitting inside their car. I calmly came out of my car. I said a little prayer and reminded myself that I cared very much for Celeste, and then I walked towards the front office.

Celeste's mom met me near the entrance of the school and told me she was there to meet as I had requested. I invited her to my office, and she said we would be holding this meeting in the parking lot. I told her that would be fine, and we proceeded to talk. I gave her the opportunity to tell me what was on her mind. I explained the series of situations that had occurred. Celeste's mom said that Celeste had always had behavior issues because she was constantly angry. She had already decided she would be taking Celeste to another school that would give her a fresh start. She had heard of a military school where Celeste could participate in a program where she would live on campus for a few months. She thanked me for being the only principal and only school to have cared for Celeste. She hugged me and asked her daughter to get out of the car to also thank me and hug me too. It was totally not what I had expected, but this story reinforced my commitment to continue to care for our students and their parents.

As you can see from this story, parents' and their children's stories are tightly interwoven.

Increasingly, schools are reporting very difficult meetings with parents. The more affluent the student population you have, the more time you will spend with parents. The higher the percentage of the student population living in poverty, the more time you will spend with students.

Historically, schools have always dealt with parents from a behavioral/cognitive approach. More and more, this does not work. For most parents, parenting is an emotional issue and highly developed from their own experience and stories.

This chapter recommends looking at parents and the emotional realities of parenting/caregiving from a brain-system approach.

But first, please examine implicit bias and institutional bias.

Implicit bias is the judgments made by the brain at the subconscious level that the conscious mind often does not know it is making. Implicit bias becomes a factor in our decision-making about the person and/or situation. Explicit bias is our conscious understanding of what our biases are.[138]

The majority of research on implicit bias is done with issues of race. There is research about implicit bias in media and how media is manipulated. There is very little implicit bias research done on issues of socioeconomic class.

Bias indicators on the part of both teacher and parent:

Area of bias	Good	View as desirable	View as less desirable
Eyes (look at you, look away, etc.)			
Educational attainment level/vocabulary			
Race (same as you, not a member of the dominant race/culture/ethnicity/ country of origin/religion, etc.)			
Gender			
Appearance (cleanliness, smell, hair)			
Body 'tells' (anxious, comfortable)			
Emotional status (fear, anger, joy)			
Energy (lethargic, high energy)			
Weight			
Age			
Ableness or disability			
Physical fitness			
Occupation			
Shoes/boots			
Clothes/jewelry			
Dialect/speech/language			

What Decisions Did I Make?

There are all kinds of bias—this person is not educated, this person is a minority, this person does not speak English, etc. Basically, what happens in bias is that the person is made "less than" or "separate from" before the person is ever known. When that happens, particularly if the bias is negative, then the mind tends not to consider options in decision-making that might change the outcome.

What Do Parents See When They Look at the Educator?

Parents often have a bias against the educator before they ever walk in the door. Using the chart above, what does the parent see when they meet you?

In the article "5 Things Parents Wish Teachers Knew for Conferences," some of the issues that upset parents are identified:

1. "I don't know educationese." In other words, education has language: IEP, ARD, Common Core math, credits, formative assessment, standards, etc. Use plain language, tangible examples, and sample work assignments.

2. "I am not the teacher, I am the parent." When a teacher indicates that the parent is to help the child, it is frustrating often because parents have a job, their own life, etc. Please remember that parents are not "bad" because they allow their child to fail or do not check every paper.

3. "I don't like it when you teach my child your political, religious, or social opinions as if they were undisputed facts."

4. "Don't surprise me." For example, I don't want to find out at the end of the six weeks that no assignments have been turned in.

5. "I love my child. Please watch what you say to me about my child."[139]

Institutional Bias

The Oxford Reference website defines institutional bias as a "tendency for the procedures and practices of particular institutions to operate in ways which result in certain social groups being advantaged or favored and others being disadvantaged or devalued."[140]

Here are some questions that indicate institutional bias:

1. How welcome are parents in this institution? Are they viewed as a necessary evil, a threat, idiots, partners, or pains in the butt?

2. Which students get the best teachers?

3. Where do the resources go in a school district?

4. How am I greeted when I walk onto the campus or call the campus?

5. Who is on the PTA? What is the mix of class and race?

6. At the elementary level, are men/fathers in attendance?

7. What activities are available on Saturday? For parents who work two jobs?

8. How are parents kept informed?

9. What is the mix of class and race on the school board?

10. How many teachers are people of color?

11. Does the curriculum include books, stories, etc. of immigrants, people of color, et al.?

12. What do the posters in the building represent?

13. At the secondary level, who is on the student council?

14. What do the discipline stats indicate?

15. Who is in the gifted program? In special education?

16. Are the procedures for due process given to every student?

17. At secondary, who is in in-school suspension? Mostly males?[141]

A Process for Building Relationships with Parents

Ruben Perez uses this process when he works with parents.

STEP ONE: The first step is to lower defenses. These are the kinds of statements/ questions that can be made: I know you love and care about your child or you would not have come to see me. What can I do so that you know that I care about your child? You know your child better than anyone. What do you know about your child that I would not know?

STEP TWO: Open up arenas to find solutions. In this step, the problem is identified, and possible solutions are examined. "If you were ruler of the universe, how would you like to see this problem solved?"

STEP THREE: Identify the steps to take. It helps if this is in writing.

In each step, you are using invitational language and doing active listening.

Invitational language includes phrases like:

Can you help me understand…

I wonder…

I noticed…

How could we…

How might…

Does it…

Will it…

What can I do for you now?

In what ways might we…

Now, what I see us doing is…

It could be even better…

I am curious…

In our continuing work with this…

Using -*ing* verbs indicates a process. For example: "What I am learning now… As we are discussing the possibilities…"

Stay away from *but*. Use *and, yet, until now.*

According to Noam Chomsky, *not* is not recognized or is skipped over by the subconscious. What is recorded in the mind is the rest of the statement without the not. For example, "We do *not* run in school" may be recorded in the mind as "We run in the school." Make statements in the positive whenever possible.

Active listening can often involve paraphrasing. There are three types of paraphrases: (a) Acknowledge the statement and clarify it: "If I understand correctly, you wish to have your child enrolled in this program. Was this to be done now?" (b) organize the information and summarize, and (c) shift the conceptual focus: "If I understand correctly, the real issue is the difficulty that is happening with…"

How Information and Stories Get Distorted

This is increasingly an issue because of the reliance on social media for information. A parent will call or come up to school and say, "I saw this on Facebook…"

One of the issues that schools are dealing with now is getting a clean story with facts. These are the ways that information can be distorted:

1. Omission – key facts or contrary details are omitted.
2. Expert selection – quoting only the experts who share your bias.
3. Commission – when inaccurate facts are used to support assumptions.
4. Story selection – which stories do you tell?
5. Beginning and ending stories – the beginning and ending stories are remembered the most.

Few individuals will include details or information that lessen the value of someone they love.

The Parent-Teacher Conference

Parent-teacher conferences and calls should be planned *before* they occur. Here is a checklist that can be used:

PARENT-TEACHER CONFERENCE FORM WITH STUDENT

Student name _____

Parent name _____ Date _____ Time _____

Teacher _____

How will the conference be conducted?   In person   Online   On the phone

---

PURPOSE OF THE CONFERENCE (CHECK AS MANY AS APPLY)

_____ scheduled parent-teacher conference

_____ student achievement issue

_____ parent-initiated

_____ discipline issue

_____ social/emotional issue

WHAT IS THE DESIRED GOAL OF THE CONFERENCE?

WHAT DATA WILL I OR THE STUDENT SHOW THE PARENT?

Student work, discipline referrals, student planning documents?

WHAT QUESTIONS NEED TO BE ASKED? WHAT ISSUES NEED TO BE DISCUSSED?

WHAT FOLLOW-UP TOOLS AND STRATEGIES WILL BE IDENTIFIED?

In Chapter 3 of the first *Emotional Poverty* book, there is a detailed discussion of bonding and attachment styles and their effects on student behavior. When you are working with parents, the bonding and attachment style may be important to consider. The following chart is from *Emotional Poverty*. Stosny, a researcher and clinician, works with men who batter women. He indicates that the disorganized (safe and dangerous) style of attachment is disproportionately represented among that population.[142]

Four Bonding and Attachment Styles

(Combination of research of Bowlby, Ainsworth, and Stosny)

Secure and attached	Insecure, anxious-ambivalent
Child's sense of self is integrated and secure • Are not easily influenced by peers • Tend to do better academically • Form healthy relationships • Brain tends to be integrated and regulated • Respond to traditional discipline techniques *"I'm lovable and you will find my love worth having."*[143]	Child's sense of self is confused • Very anxious in the classroom • Often easily bullied • Difficulty with boundaries in relationships • Do not always do the work because it might not be right • Need repeated assurances • Self is to blame if there is a relationship problem *"I'm not lovable, but you are so loving that I will do anything to get you to stay/like me."*[144]
Insecure, anxious-avoidant	**Disorganized (safe and dangerous)**
Child's sense of self is disconnected • Tend to be loners • Difficulty with forming relationships • Are restricted emotionally • Avoid assignments that require an emotional response • Peers often do not like them • Do not respond to typical discipline techniques *"I am unlovable and you'll reject me anyway, so why bother."*[145]	Child's sense of self is fragmented, unregulated, and unintegrated • Operate out of fear and anger • Cannot name their emotions • Have parents who are often safe and dangerous and tend to rage when angry • Few boundaries, little attachment • Do not respond to typical discipline techniques • Need development of regulation and inner strengths *"I'm lovable, but you're either too insensitive to see it or you're just not worthy of my love."*[146]

These are key questions that should be determined about the parents *before* interventions are recommended or determined:

Behavior	Look for	Importance	Strategy
Where is the parent in relation to the development of the prefrontal cortex (decision-making, executive function, planning, self-control, impulse control)?	Quickness to anger, intense mood swings, inability to identify a plan or steps to take. Lots of blame or victimization language.	There is no point in suggesting interventions that are not going to happen.	Ask these questions: How might this issue be resolved or solved? If you were ruler of the universe, what would you want to see happen? What accountability measures might we use?
How stressed is the parent? If the parent is really stressed, the prefrontal cortex will not function as well.	Fidgeting. Bouncing or shifting their feet. Eyes down, shoulders slumped indicates negativity. No smiles.	You need to know how much of the prefrontal cortex is being used and where and how to begin conversations.	Find a way to get the parent to relax (offer coffee or water, for example). Say: You know your child better than I do. What should I know that would help us? (Stress is often related to a lack of control. This statement allows parents to feel that they are more in control.)
As you watch their limbic system "tells," what is their level of comfort in your office? Do they want to run? Are they angry? Do they soothe themselves?	Do they turn away from you when you speak to them? Do they evade conversation? Do they close or rub their eyes or cover their face with their hands? Do they lean away or turn their feet toward the exit?	This will determine how much they are willing to be a participant in the issue, conversation, or plan regarding their child.	Do not posture with the parent. This could provoke a more intense situation. Remain open with your body language, and use invitational language such as, "I wonder if you can help me…" "How can I help and support you…?" "I noticed…"

(continued on next page)

(continued from previous page)

Behavior	Look for	Importance	Strategy
What are the limbic system "tells" when they discuss their child? How do they really feel about their child? How much do they know about their child? (The average parent spends seven minutes a day talking to their child.)	Are they open and using hand gestures? Do they make eye contact or look away? Do the speak about their child positively or negatively? Do they know their child's likes, dislikes, goals, dreams, etc.?	If they do not like their child or do not know much about the child, your interventions will be different. If the parent shows up, you know that there is caring for the child or they would not have come.	Children bring out intense feelings. Ask: What does your child do well? What have you noticed about your child that is unique to them? In what ways is your child a challenge? What approach would you recommend for your child for this issue?
Is this parent into psychological control, behavioral control, or neither?	Are they attempting to manipulate the situation? Are they attempting to manipulate you? Do they want to blame you entirely for any negative situation?	It is easy to get caught in an unproductive web where we play victim, bully, or rescuer.	Stay out of the drama triangle! Answer questions with questions.
What style of bonding and attachment does the parent seem to exhibit with their child?	How does the child act when they enter the room with their parent present? How does the parent speak to the child?	Understanding the bonding and attachment style will help you determine what intervention to use.	Use "we" statements. Use invitational language when discussing a plan for moving forward.
What is the narrative or story the parent brings to the child and to themselves as a parent? What are the stories they carry from their own parents?	What does the parent talk about (food, money, goals)? Are they proactive or reactive in nature? Do they live in perpetual triage, or do they have a plan?	This will determine how much they are willing to be a participant in the issue, conversation, or plan regarding their child.	What is the most important thing a parent can do for their child? When you think about how you were parented, is there anything you would like to do differently with your child?

Chart developed by Jen Nehl.

About 10% of your parents will be "frequent flyers." You will see them a lot. Use the grid to identify them.

Checklist for Parents Who Will Require Extra Time and Intervention

One middle school principal I know works with his staff to identify who these parents are. Then, during the summer, they visit each of these parents and build relationships with them before school starts.

Do you have parents who...	Yes or no
1. Cuss you out or threaten you during the meeting?	
2. Do not want their child to experience consequences?	
3. Blame the teacher every time?	
4. Demand that their rules be used for all students?	
5. Make excuses or lie for their child?	
6. Do everything for their child?	
7. Demand special privileges for their child?	
8. Observe in the classroom and instruct the teacher?	
9. Spread gossip and stories about other students?	
10. Threaten you with their lawyer?	
11. Tell you that they called the police on their own child or that they are unable to make the child do anything?	
12. Come to a meeting drugged?	
13. Are unable to understand the situation?	
14. Encourage their child to be absent or tardy?	

Questions to Ask Parents

1. What do you think is the most important thing a parent can do for their child? This is basically an identity question. In other words, how does the parent view parenting?

2. What do you want your child to do, be, or have when they are 25? Do they have a future story for their child?

3. At what age do you think the child will be responsible for themself? This question is checking when they will give their child personal responsibility.

4. As a parent, what would you like to do, be, or have for your child that your parents did not do, model, or provide for you? This is a key question because many times parenting is done in reaction to the way the person was parented. It tells you the priority the parent has for parenting.

5. One of the most common issues in parenting is getting enough sleep. Has that been hard to do? Not getting enough sleep can be tied to mood swings, depression, decision-making, etc.

A Story

Written by Michael Curl, a middle school principal in Texas

One of the most nerve-racking parts of our work is entering the world of the unknown when it comes to parents wanting to meet without us knowing what we are getting ourselves into. Or worse, having to come in after problematic email conversations have already been had with a staff member, and now we will be expected to mend the relationship. The more prepared and confident the school person is when going into the meeting the better. We have found that discussing bonding and attachment styles makes a significant difference in the responses of our staff to different types of parents.

One example is a set of parents I met who had been excitable in the past. So much so that teachers had been dismissed from the conference because the conversation was so uncomfortable between the now-divorced parents. The father was upset about how poorly his son was doing in school and was adamant that he be held back a grade. The school team felt the student had made agreeable progress and did not deem it appropriate to hold him back. The father was loud, demeaning, and intent on making the decision even though there were five other adults in the room who disagreed with him. When he contacted us about meeting again this year after becoming very upset about his son's failing grades, the staff became apprehensive when reflecting on the meeting from last year.

What was different this time was that many of the staff present had been provided information on bonding and attachment styles, as well as other factors that affect emotional development. By meeting beforehand to name and speak on what we may encounter, we were able to discuss parenting styles that were displayed in the two households, as well as things we could discuss with the parents to address their concerns. The student spent time with both parents, and they had different ways of interacting with him at home. By better preparing the staff, we were able to move from the common "he's just not doing the work" narrative that happens in so many parent conferences to a discussion on the outside-of-the-classroom factors that were affecting him. We were able to name and address the emotional dance that was occurring in class as a result of things outside of our building. The meeting ended up going well because the staff felt confident and cohesive going in, and that made them more at ease to make sound decisions and provide poignant feedback to both parents.

Some of Your Parents Are Not Available

Parents may be unavailable because they are incarcerated, traveling, mentally or physically ill, addicted, etc. What do you do about parents who are unavailable?

If the parent is not available, teach the child how to parent themself. Put them with a mentor if possible.

For All Parents: Stay Out of the Triangle[147]

What is the triangle? For one thing, it is deadly. If you have a tendency to fall into one of the three roles, that can encourage other people involved in the conflict to take on the other roles in response.

The same person can take on all three roles in different situations. In one setting the person is a bully, in another setting the person is a rescuer, and in another setting the person is a victim. Once you are in the triangle, you will eventually take on all three roles—and boundaries disappear because ownership isn't taken by anyone.

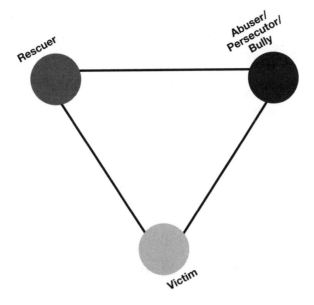

To stay out of the triangle, you can ask questions. Here's an example of using questions to avoid the triangle:

When I was a principal, I had a father of a fourth-grade girl named Kate come to me and say, "My daughter is being sexually harassed by Brandon. You will promise me that Brandon will never speak to her again."

I said to him, "I take sexual harassment very seriously, and I appreciate you coming to see me. I am required by law to give every child due process. The first thing that must be done is to separate out the facts. Can you tell me, what is Brandon doing and saying? What does Kate do when he does those things?"

The father said, "I don't know," so we called Kate in, and I asked her what Brandon was saying and doing. She told me. Then I said to her, "When he does that, what do you do?"

She said, "I just smile."

I thought her father was going to have a fit! I said, "You must tell him that you do not like that." (Keep in mind that these children are 10 years old and are just beginning to understand how to interact socially.)

She said, "I cannot do that."

Her father said, "Yes, you can."

I sent Kate back to her classroom, and I said to the father, "I am going to deal with Brandon. A key issue here is how to teach Kate to protect herself in situations like these. She is going to have unwanted advances all of her life. What will you do when she is in high school and the situation may involve sexual assault or rape? Don't you think it would be very important for Kate to have some skills as well?"

The father said, "Absolutely. I will talk with her."

Then I said to the father, "I will work with Brandon. I want you to call me if anything happens again. We do not want this on our campus."

By asking questions, I stayed out of the triangle.

Staying Out of Emotional Manipulation[148]

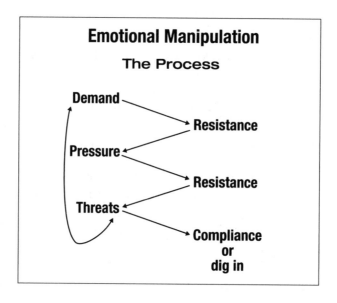

Emotional manipulation, or emotional blackmail, is a common practice. The word *blackmail* comes from the 13th century, when rogue soldiers did not clean their metal armor.

In the book *Emotional Blackmail,* the author identifies the process people use to force another individual to do what they wish. It always starts out with a demand.[149]

Person A *makes a demand.* "I want you to change my child's grade to an A from a B."

Person B *resists.* "I am not going to change the grade because the student did not earn an A."

Person A *adds pressure.* "You know that teacher is not competent. She was out sick for two weeks. It is not fair to jeopardize my child because of an incompetent teacher."

Person B *resists.* "The substitute we had in that classroom is a retired teacher who is excellent. These grades actually came from formative assessments."

Person A *threatens.* "I am going to go to the superintendent or a school board member (whom I know personally) to explain how biased and unfair this situation is."

Person B *complies.* "You know, I think we can find a way to change their grade."

Before you get involved in this process, you need to stop the process at the first demand by asking the following kinds of questions. Each question uses the word *specific* or *specifically.*

"Specifically, what did your child do to earn an A? Can you give me specific examples? Can we ask the teacher for specific copies of your child's work?"

Stay away from the word *why*—it puts people on the defensive. Ask these kinds of questions: "Specifically, when? Specifically, how? To what extent? Where, specifically, did that occur? What happened, specifically?"

Parent Engagement

In the parent engagement research, parents coming up to school makes no difference in student achievement. What does make a difference is when the parent provides expectations (they know where their children are at night and whether they have homework), insistence, and support.

Niche market to your parents. One size does not fit all.

Niche Marketing to Parents

Niche marketing is a term used in advertising. Simply put, it means that one size does not fit all and that marketing needs to be targeted at specific audiences. The following table outlines some of the subgroups of parents found in many schools and ideas for involvement in their child's education. *A parent does not need to come to school to be involved.*

Put these activities into the site-based plan so that they occur. The activities actually become a marketing plan for the campus.

Subgroups of parents	Ideas for involvement
Two-career parents	Put many things in print, e.g., fliers, newsletters, web pages, etc. These parents will read and keep informed. Ask for email addresses, and send a monthly or weekly email that updates them on the classroom and school activities.
Involved parents	These parents are at school, volunteering their help. The issue here is overinvolvement and parents wanting to take on administrative roles. Sometimes the boundaries involving student privacy need to be revisited.
Nonworking and uninvolved parents	This occurs at both ends of the economic spectrum. Phone banks where parents call parents and tell them about school activities begin a network. Home contacts are very powerful, as are coffee klatches.
Surrogate parents	These are grandparents, foster parents, et al. They often need emotional support. Assign them a mentor—e.g., a counselor or involved parent—who touches base with them once a month.
Immigrant parents	Make short videos dubbed in their own language explaining how school works, how to talk to the teacher, what grades mean, what homework means, etc. Have the videos made by a person in your community from that immigrant group. *Do not make them too slick or professional* because they will not be believed.
Parents working two jobs	Color-code the information you send home. White paper is "nice to know." Yellow paper indicates a concern. Red paper means that immediate attention is needed. You can call these parents at work as long as you do not talk at that time; ask them to call you back. Videos to introduce the teacher work well also.
Single parents	Structure activities that make life easier for the parent, activities that would include the children or childcare, food (so they don't need to cook), or activities scheduled on the weekends or with open time frames rather than specific meeting times. Videos to introduce the teacher also work well here.

(continued on next page)

(continued from previous page)

Subgroups of parents	Ideas for involvement
Parents who are unavailable and students who, in effect, are their own parents	These are parents who are incarcerated, mentally ill, physically ill, travel a great deal, immigrants who have returned to their native country or been deported, have an addiction, etc. Teach the student how to be their own parent. Provide linkages for the student to other school service agencies. Have the counselor have "what if" lunches where pizza is brought in, and have four or five other students in this same situation discuss issues.
Parents who are "crazy makers"	There are only a few of these in a building (fewer than 1%), but they destroy time and energy. They have two characteristics—they take lots of time, and the situation can never be resolved. They talk to everyone and involve multiple personnel and take *hours of time.* They get the time because they threaten to go to the superintendent or the board. Talk to your supervisor about these individuals and how much time should be given to them.

A part of site-based planning is to identify the percentages of parents who fit into these categories. If you have many parents in one subgroup, then it would be important to address more of those involvement issues.

Building Communities of Support

The layering and structuring of "practices that contribute to student engagement and high school completion" is the basic concept in communities of support. "Chief among these is the ability of school personnel to create communities of support that are concerned about how students perform and express that concern in genuine, effective, caring ways."[150] So how does one do that?

One way is to create a scaffolding of interventions. The other is by creating linkages to community groups. The following suggestions can help create communities of support for parents:

a) **Mutual respect:** Parents are welcomed by first-line staff. Parents are welcome in the building. Accusatory and blaming language is not present.

b) **School design teams:** A cross-section of staff, parents, law enforcement, ministers, and students who identify issues of support.

c) **Home contacts:** These are not home visits but quick five-minute visits to the home at the beginning of school to say hello. Substitutes are used to release teachers to do this.

d) **Videos:** These can be made by the staff and students to introduce faculty, to tell about school discipline programs, to highlight upcoming events, etc.

e) **Student and parent voices:** Through informal conversation (not meetings), parents and students are asked what the school could do to better serve them.

f) **Weekend activities:** Friday evenings, Saturday mornings, and Sunday afternoons work the best.

g) **Varied and targeted parental involvement activities:** Free donuts for dads the first Monday of every month. Carnations for moms. Lunch for grandparents. Picnics for people who live in the student's house.

h) **Support mechanisms for parents that involve follow-up:** 3 x 5 cards with the steps that will be followed. Magnets for the refrigerator that list school phone numbers and holidays. Stickers that parents can give to the child for good behaviors.

i) **Informal coffee klatches:** Counselor or principal asks a parent with whom they already have a relationship to invite three or four other friends over for coffee in the parent's home. The principal or counselor brings the donuts. This is a forum for an informal discussion about what bothers parents, what they would like to see, what they like, etc.

j) **Overcoming reluctance to participate by creating one-on-one relationships.**

k) **Tools for dealing with parent-teacher conferences.**

l) **Tools for dealing with difficult parents.**

m) **Simple written documents that have pictures and words and/or cartoons.**

n) Using networking capabilities in the community: Make a flier with cartoons that is one page and has an advertisement for a business in the community on the back. Introduce your faculty through cartoons. The advertiser pays for the paper and the printing. Distribute them to beauty salons, grocery stores, barbershops, churches, etc., much like a local community shopper or merchandiser.

o) Information for parents that enhances their lives: Offer information like how to fix bad credit (knowledge about money), how to manage a difficult boss (conflict resolution skills), etc.

p) Information on video or in cartoon that helps parents deal with their children, e.g., how to enhance obedience in your child.

q) Giving awards to parents: A child identifies something a parent has done. On a Saturday morning, the child gives a certificate to the parent and thanks the parent.

r) Parent-teacher conferences led by the student.

s) Weekend activities that use the computers and athletic facilities of the campus.

t) Partner with a campus that has a surplus of parent involvement.

u) Peer-mediation training for students: They teach it to parents informally.

v) Teaching students to be better friends: Have students list the five friends they go to when they have a problem. Tally who are the "best friends." Teach them how to ask questions to solve problems. Teach them how to identify which problems are serious and need to be referred, such as threats of suicide.

w) Teaching parents to be better friends to other adults.

x) Block parties: Get a street blocked off for an afternoon and have a party.

In other words, creating communities of support is a layered, varied set of interventions and activities. The idea that a school can have X number of meetings a year, a carnival, and a Halloween party is not enough. What must occur is a scaffolding of interventions.

Working with Parents from Poverty

The first issue to address when working with parents from poverty is mutual respect. The second is the use of casual register. The third is the way discipline is used in the household. The fourth is the way time is viewed. And the fifth is the role of school and education in their lives.

First, for many parents in generational poverty, school is not given a high priority. It is often feared and resented. Their own personal experience may not have been positive, and school is alternately viewed as a babysitter or a necessary evil (e.g., "If I don't send my child, I will have to go to court"). Second, when parents come in, because of their heavy reliance on a win/lose approach to conflict, they may begin with an in-your-face approach. Remember, they are doing this, consciously or unconsciously, as a show of strength. Just stay in the adult voice. Use language that is clear and straightforward. If you use "educationese," they're likely to think you're trying to cheat or trick them.

Use these kinds of phrases with parents from poverty (these are the types of comments they often use with their own children):

- "Learning this will help your child win more often."
- "The mind is a mental weapon that no one can take from you."
- "If you do this, your child will be smarter and won't get cheated or tricked."
- "Learning this will help your child make more money."
- "This information will help keep your child safer."
- "I know you love and care about your child very much or you wouldn't be here" (but don't say this if you don't mean it).

Discipline in generational poverty vacillates from being very permissive to very punitive. The emotional mood of the moment often determines what occurs. Also, in some cultures, the approach to boys is very different from the approach to girls. When the discipline is highly punitive, there is often a belief system that (a) the harsher the punishment, the greater the forgiveness, and (b) the harsher punishment will make the young person stronger and tougher.

Consequently, the notion of a systematic approach to discipline usually doesn't exist. There is rarely mediation or intervention about a behavior. Generally, it is a slap and a "quit that." If guidance is being provided to the parent about behavior, use a what, why, how approach with visuals.

Tips for Working with Parents from Poverty

- Many adults from poverty didn't have a positive school experience. The greeting of the first staff member they encounter (secretary, aide, administrator, teacher) will either confirm their earlier experience or counter it. Some sort of building procedure and greeting should be agreed upon.

- Always call them by Mr. or Mrs. (unless told otherwise). It's a sign of respect.

- Identify your intent. Intent determines nonverbals. Parents from poverty decide whether they like you based largely on your nonverbals. If they don't like you, they won't support you or work with you. For example, if your intent is to win, that will be reflected in your nonverbals. Likewise, if your intent is to understand, that will be reflected as well.

- Use humor (not sarcasm). They particularly look to see if you have a sense of humor about yourself. For example: Can you tell a story about yourself in which you weren't the hero? Can you poke fun at yourself?

- Deliver bad news through a story. If you state the bad news directly (e.g., your son was stealing), it will invite an automatic defense of the child. Instead, say, "Let me tell you a story. Maybe you can help me with the situation." Make sure you use the word *story.*

- If you're comfortable using casual register, use it. If not, don't use it. They'll probably think you're making fun of them.

- Be human, and don't be afraid to indicate you don't have all the answers. As alluded to above, they distrust anyone who is "always the hero of their own stories."

- Offer a cup of coffee. In poverty, coffee is frequently offered as a sign of welcome.

- Use the adult voice. Be understanding but firm. Be open to discussion, but don't change the consequences (unless new information surfaces or a better solution can be found).

- Be personally strong. You aren't respected in generational poverty unless you are personally strong. If you're threatened or have an in-your-face encounter, don't show fear. You don't need to be mean. Just don't show fear.

- If parents are angry, they may appeal to physical power ("I'm going to beat you up!"). To calm them, say, "I know you love and care about your child very much or you wouldn't be here. What can we do that would show we also care?" Another phrase that often works is: "Are you mad at me, or are you just mad?"

- Use videos as a way to provide information and communicate with parents. Virtually every U.S. home in poverty has a TV and DVD player. If possible, make the videos entertaining. They can be in any language, but they should be short.

- Story structure in generational poverty is episodic and random, and the discourse pattern is circular. Understand that these structures take much longer. Allow enough time during conferences for these structures to be used.

- Home visits by teachers are the fastest and easiest way to build a huge parent support base quickly. They also significantly reduce discipline issues. Use Title I money to pay teachers to make phone calls and do home visits before there is a problem. (The payoff from this one simple activity is tremendous.)

- Remember, the parents from poverty talked about you in the neighborhood before they came to see you. They often made outrageous comments about what they were going to say and do to you before they went to the school (entertainment is an important part of the culture of poverty). So when they return to the neighborhood, they have to report back. Some comments you may end up hearing will be so outrageous that they should be ignored. They were made because they told people in the neighborhood they were going to do so.

- As you discuss situations with parents, ask yourself what resources are available to these individuals. Some suggestions won't work because the resources simply aren't available.

- In middle class, when a topic is introduced that the individual doesn't want to discuss, they will simply change the subject. In generational poverty, the individual often tells the person what they want to hear, particularly if that person is in a position of authority.

- Emphasize that there are two sets of rules: one set for school and work, another set for outside of school and work.

- Don't accept behaviors from adults that you don't accept from students.

Tips for Working with Parents from Wealth

- Don't use humor—at least initially—when discussing their child or situation. If you do, they'll think you don't care about them or their child.

- One of the hidden rules in affluence is: "It's not okay not to be perfect." Identifying your personal weaknesses will not appeal to them particularly. They want to know that you are very good at what you do. On the other hand, if you don't know something, don't try to bluff your way through. They will usually call your bluff.

- Another hidden rule in affluence is that you aren't respected unless you're able to discriminate by quality or artistic merit. Wealthy parents won't respect you unless you have expertise. If you aren't knowledgeable in a particular area, read the experts or get a school district expert to sit in with you for the meeting.

- Don't use circular discourse or casual register. They want to get straight to the point and discuss the issue through formal register. They won't respect you if you waste their time.

- Do use the adult voice with affluent parents. Understand that they are skilled negotiators. Clearly establish parameters when discussing issues with them. Affluent parents often believe that they and their children don't need to follow or adhere to the "rules" of the organization. Be firm about those boundaries.

- Emphasize issues of safety, legal parameters, and the need for the student to develop coping mechanisms for greater success later in life.

- Understand that a primary motivator for wealthy parents is the financial, social, and academic success of their child. They're very interested in what you'll be able to do to help their child be successful.

- When affluent parents come to school and are upset, they likely will appeal to positional power, financial power, or connections ("I know the school board president"…"I'll call my lawyer"…). They also will attack the issues. Be prepared to articulate the issues, and use experts by name in the discussion.

- Don't be intimidated by the affluent parent. Do understand, regardless of your position, who is standing behind you to support you. If you have little or no support above you, make sure you don't paint yourself into a corner. Affluent parents will "rattle the organizational cage" in order to get what they want.

- Understand the competitive nature of wealth (especially among those with "new money") and the need to excel. Their children are expected to be the best. There tends to be disrespect for those in the service sector, including public service. However, if their child is happy and doing well, most of them will be incredibly supportive.

Dealing with Parents Who Are Too Involved

When I was a principal, I found out that my teachers were hanging up on parents when they called. This particular elementary school was very affluent. So I told my staff that we could not do that because when we needed help, we would not want them to hang up on us. In the discussion that followed, what was revealed is that the parents did the following: criticized the teacher in front of the students, talked about children other than their own in the neighborhood, demanded information on children who were not their children that they had no legal right to know, and created problems. I explained to the staff that two of those issues violated the Family Educational Rights and Privacy Act. So we asked each parent volunteer to sign the following document:

Contract for Classroom Volunteers

In order to protect my own child, I agree to the following guidelines:

1. I will not discuss any child other than my own outside of the school and/or the classroom. To do so is to violate the Family Educational Rights and Privacy Act.
2. I will not criticize the teacher in front of the students.
3. I will not ask for confidential data about any student other than my own.
4. If I have a problem with something a teacher does, I can talk to the teacher privately. If I still am unsatisfied, I can talk to the principal about it.

I agree to these guidelines in order to protect my own child. If I do not follow these guidelines, I may be asked not to volunteer again.

_____

Signature

Chapter Summary

1. Parenting is an emotional activity. People tend to parent either based on the way they were parented or in reaction to the way they were parented.

2. Implicit bias on the part of both the educator and the parent impacts the working relationship with a parent.

3. Institutional biases in a district or campus that a parent might witness also impact the process of working together.

4. Using the process of lowering defenses, finding the arenas of solutions, and coming to a solution through invitational language and active listening promote better outcomes.

5. Using the Karpman triangle to solve problems and find solutions tends to eliminate blame, accusations, and rescuing.

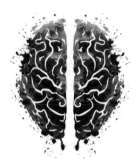

Conclusion

What We Can Do

1. We can help students identify what their bodies are telling them.

2. We can more quickly identify from students' bodily "tells" what their emotional state is.

3. We can facilitate the development of the prefrontal cortex, especially social cognition and perspective-taking, in middle and secondary students.

4. We can facilitate the development of coherent stories in students.

5. We can lower the stress level in adults by identifying the indicators of stress in the body.

6. We can be more effective with parents by examining the emotional underpinnings of the issues.

This book contains just some of the ways educators can work to achieve emotional stability in their students and in themselves. The journey to safer, calmer schools isn't over. Thank you for the progress you make every day. I hope the insights and strategies shared here help make the road a little smoother and the trip a little faster for everyone in our schools.

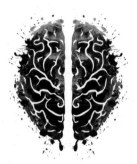

Endnotes

[1] L. Wittgenstein, *Tractatus Logico-Philosophicus*
[2] J. Navarro, *What Every Body Is Saying*
[3] *Ibid.*
[4] *Ibid.*
[5] *Ibid.*, p. 68
[6] *Ibid.*, p. 72
[7] *Ibid.*, p. 101
[8] *Ibid.*, pp. 112–114
[9] *Ibid.*, p. 118
[10] *Ibid.*, p. 134
[11] *Ibid.*
[12] *Ibid.*, p. 176
[13] A. Loyd, *The Love Code*
[14] *Ibid.*
[15] *Ibid.*
[16] A. Loyd, *The Success Codes*
[17] *Ibid.*, p. 25
[18] HeartMath Institute, "Energetic Communication"
[19] HeartMath Institute, "Coherence"
[20] HeartMath Institute, "Energetic Communication"
[21] S. Jain et al., "Clinical Studies of Biofield Therapies"
[22] B. Schulte, "Harvard Neuroscientist: Meditation Not Only Reduces Stress, Here's How It Changes Your Brain"
[23] *Ibid.*
[24] M. Eisler, "What's the Difference Between Meditation and Mindfulness?"
[25] A. Loyd, *The Truth Technique*
[26] L. Curran, *101 Trauma-Informed Interventions*
[27] *Ibid.*
[28] H. Crockett, personal correspondence
[29] J. Giedd, "The Teen Brain"
[30] S.-J. Blakemore, *Inventing Ourselves*
[31] D. Amen, *Change Your Brain, Change Your Life*, pp. 8–14
[32] *Ibid.*, p. 18
[33] *Ibid.*, p. 191
[34] *Ibid.*

[35] A. Arnsten, "Stress Signaling Pathways That Impair Prefrontal Cortex Structure and Function"

[36] C. Pittman and E. Karle, *Rewire Your Anxious Brain*

[37] J. Ledoux and J. Gorman, "A Call to Action"

[38] C. Pittman and E. Karle, *Rewire Your Anxious Brain*

[39] *Ibid.*

[40] *Ibid.*, p. 38

[41] Ibid., p. 113

[42] R. C. Clark, *Building Expertise*

[43] Association of American Educators, "Character Education Programs"

[44] T. Srebro, "Doing Good Can Make You Feel Good, Study on Volunteerism Finds"

[45] R. K. Payne, *Achievement for All*

[46] *Ibid.*

[47] *Ibid.*

[48] J. Peterson, *12 Rules for Life*

[49] *Ibid.*

[50] *Ibid.*

[51] Wikipedia, "Sex and Gender Distinction"

[52] T. Jewell, "How Long Does It Take for Sperm to Regenerate?"

[53] A. Targonskaya, "How Many Eggs Do Women Have?"

[54] A. Pietrangelo, "The Effects of Testosterone on the Body"

[55] B. Brookshire, "Hormone Affects How Teens' Brains Control Emotions"

[56] C. Pickhardt, "Puberty and Preoccupation with Personal Appearance"

[57] How Youth Learn, "The Teenage Brain"

[58] *Ibid.*

[59] M. Arain et al., "Maturation of the Adolescent Brain"

[60] *Ibid.*

[61] J. Giedd, "The Digital Revolution and Adolescent Brain Evolution"

[62] *Ibid.*

[63] M. Walker, *Why We Sleep*

[64] M. Arain et al., "Maturation of the Adolescent Brain"

[65] National Institute on Drug Abuse, "Understanding Drug Abuse and Addiction"

[66] Fight the New Drug, "How Porn Affects the Brain Like a Drug"

[67] *Ibid.*

[68] M. Arain et al., "Maturation of the Adolescent Brain"

[69] *Ibid.*

[70] *Ibid.*

[71] J. Beck, "How Pornography Affects Teenagers [and Children]"

[72] Fight the New Drug, "How Watching Porn Can Mess with Your Brain—Literally"

[73] *Ibid.*

[74] Fight the New Drug, "Can Watching Porn Actually Be Healthy for You?"

[75] S. Adelson et al., "Toward a Definition of 'Hypersexuality' in Children and Adolescents"

[76] Fight the New Drug, "Love Is Natural. Porn Is Produced."

[77] J. Giedd, "The Digital Revolution and Adolescent Brain Evolution"

[78] *Ibid.*

[79] *Ibid.*

[80] M. Arain et al., "Maturation of the Adolescent Brain"

[81] *Ibid.*

[82] *Ibid.*

[83] ScienceDirect, "Social Cognition"

[84] S. Choudhury et al., "Social Cognitive Development During Adolescence"

[85] *Ibid.*

[86] R. K. Payne, *Achievement for All*

[87] S. Choudhury et al., "Social Cognitive Development During Adolescence"

[88] *Ibid.*

[89] J. M. Jose, "Teaching Morality: Kohlberg's Theory of Moral Development"

[90] J. Galbraith, "The Eight Great Gripes of Gifted Kids"; A. Roeper, "Should Educators of the Gifted and Talented Be More Concerned with World Issues?"; L. K. Silverman, "Social Development, Leadership, and Gender Issues" and "The Moral Sensitivity of Gifted Children and the Evolution of Society."

[91] S. Choudhury et al., "Social Cognitive Development During Adolescence"

[92] B. Chhetry et al., "Omega-3 Polyunsaturated Fatty Acid Supplementation and White Matter Changes in Major Depression."

[93] P. Kramer and P. Bress, "Our (Mother's) Mitochondria and Our Mind"

[94] PBS, "Interview: Jay Giedd"

[95] D. J. Siegel, *Mindsight*

[96] M. Rukeyser, "The Speed of Darkness"

[97] G. Miller, "How Our Brains Make Memories"

[98] K. McLean et al., "The Empirical Structure of Narrative Identity"

[99] K. McLean, *The Coauthored Self*

[100] *Ibid.*

[101] *Ibid.*, p. 22

[102] *Ibid.*, p. 6

[103] *Ibid.*, p. 27

[104] I. M. Cron and S. Stabile, *The Road Back to You*

[105] S. Hammel, *Handbook of Therapeutic Storytelling*, p. 97

[106] R. Solnit, *The Faraway Nearby*, p. 152

[107] M. Martinez, *The MindBody Code*

[108] R. Solnit, *The Faraway Nearby*, p. 246

[109] How Youth Learn, "The Teenage Brain"

[110] Elite HRV, "Normative Elite HRV Scores by Age and Gender"

[111] HeartMath Institute, "Heart-Brain Communication"

[112] A. Loyd, with B. Johnson, *The Healing Code*, p. 44

[113] *Ibid.*, p. 45

[114] *Ibid.*

[115] *Ibid.*

[116] *Ibid.*

[117] HeartMath Institute, "Heart Rate Variability"

[118] A. Loyd, with B. Johnson, *The Healing Code*

[119] *Ibid.*

[120] *Ibid.*

[121] *Ibid.*

[122] HeartMath Institute, "Coherence"

[123] HeartMath Institute, "Energetic Communication"

[124] HeartMath Institute, "Heart-Brain Communication"

[125] L. Curran, *101 Trauma-Informed Interventions*

[126] HeartMath Institute, "Coherence"

[127] R. Kurtus, "Noise Cancellation"

[128] R. Kurtus, "Beat Frequencies in Sound"

[129] A. Loyd, with B. Johnson, *The Healing Code*

[130] V. Rajmohan and E. Mohandas, "Mirror Neuron System"

[131] *Ibid.*

[132] F. Mathieu, *The Compassion Fatigue Workbook*, p. 8

[133] R. Warren, "10 Signs You're Emotionally Exhausted"

[134] B. Rothschild, *The Body Remembers Volume 2*

[135] A. Loyd, *The Success Codes*

[136] S. Rosenberg, *Accessing the Healing Power of the Vagus Nerve*

[137] K. McLean, *The Coauthored Self*, p. 84

[138] G. L. Gullo, K. Capatosto, and C. Staats, *Implicit Bias in Schools*

[139] M. Mathis, "5 Things Parents Wish Teachers Knew for Conferences"

[140] "Overview: Institutional Bias"

[141] G. Cassetta and M. Wilson, "Recognizing Schools' Institutional Bias"

[142] S. Stosny, *Treating Attachment Abuse,* page 21

[143] *Ibid.*, page 22

[144] *Ibid.*

[145] *Ibid.*

[146] *Ibid.*, page 61

[147] S. Karpman, "Fairy Tales and Script Drama Analysis"

[148] S. Forward, *Emotional Blackmail*

[149] *Ibid.*

[150] El Puente Project, "Helping Latino High School Youth Make Something of Themselves"

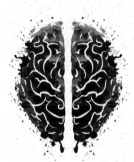

Appendix A

Professional Book Study
for Educators

Chapter 1: The Limbic Center

1. **How to watch body "tells" to determine emotional distress**
2. **How to use the energy systems of the body to reduce emotional distress**
3. **How to use these tools to keep your campus safer**

Goals for learning: (What are your professional goals or outcomes for this book study?)	
Focus questions and topics for the chapter: (Questions to answer as a group in response to the reading.)	• How do you currently handle an "in your face" explosion? • When looking at nonverbal behavior of freeze, take flight, or fight, which "tells" will you pay most attention to and why? • Can you identify some of your stories or memories that have been stored at the cellular level? How have these impacted your habits, thinking, or life? • What strategies do you currently use to calm students, adults, or even yourself?
Application to classroom practice: (What processes or information will you use or incorporate in your classroom tomorrow?)	
Reflections: (Have any thoughts, feelings, or preconceived ideas shifted due to the chapter information?)	
Next steps: (What needs to be completed prior to the next meeting/session?)	

Chapter 2: Developing the Prefrontal Cortex

- **Building regulation and emotional stability**

Goals for learning: (What are your professional goals or outcomes for this book study?)	
Focus questions and topics for the chapter: (Questions to answer as a group in response to the reading.)	▪ **What are three significant factors to understand about the prefrontal cortex?** ▪ **What happens to the prefrontal cortex when a person is stressed?** ▪ **What impact does anxiety have when trying to process and create emotional stability?** ▪ **What do you do in your district, building, or room to build integrity or emotional stability?**
Application to classroom practice: (What processes or information will you use or incorporate in your classroom tomorrow?)	
Reflections: (Have any thoughts, feelings, or preconceived ideas shifted due to the chapter information?)	
Next steps: (What needs to be completed prior to the next meeting/session?)	

Chapter 3: Adolescent Brain Development

- **What appears on the surface looks much different than what is occurring in the brain**

Goals for learning: (What are your professional goals or outcomes for this book study?)	
Focus questions and topics for the chapter: (Questions to answer as a group in response to the reading.)	▪ What are markers of social cognition in the students you work with? ▪ The job of the reward pathway is to release chemicals that give a person a rush of pleasure so they will repeat a behavior. How does this support the role peers play in adolescence? ▪ How is your school addressing the two critical issues the brain is concerned with as an adolescent: the development of social cognition and perspective-taking? ▪ What role does screen time play in how the brain rewires itself?
Application to classroom practice: (What processes or information will you use or incorporate in your classroom tomorrow?)	
Reflections: (Have any thoughts, feelings, or preconceived ideas shifted due to the chapter information?)	
Next steps: (What needs to be completed prior to the next meeting/session?)	

Chapter 4: The Hippocampus

- **Your memory and the stories you carry in your head form your identity**
- **"My experiences trump your truth." –Rickey Frierson**

Goals for learning: (What are your professional goals or outcomes for this book study?)	
Focus questions and topics for the chapter: (Questions to answer as a group in response to the reading.)	<ul><li>Which of the "big three" key features of internal stories—motivational and affective themes, autobiographical reasoning, and structure—have most impacted you?</li><li>Everyone has wounds. Does your wound define you, or has it strengthened you? How do you know?</li><li>Wherever a person has experienced a wound, that is where they stagnate cognitively. Have you stagnated? Where have your students stagnated?</li><li>What can you strategically offer your students who have a childhood wound?</li></ul>
Application to classroom practice: (What processes or information will you use or incorporate in your classroom tomorrow?)	
Reflections: (Have any thoughts, feelings, or preconceived ideas shifted due to the chapter information?)	
Next steps: (What needs to be completed prior to the next meeting/session?)	

Chapter 5: When the Adults Are Stressed

- Strategies for secondary traumatic stress or compassion fatigue in adults
- When the adults are stressed, the ability to teach is significantly reduced, as is the ability to respond with appropriate actions

Goals for learning: (What are your professional goals or outcomes for this book study?)	
Focus questions and topics for the chapter: (Questions to answer as a group in response to the reading.)	- What events cause you to feel compassion fatigue? How do you take care of yourself during these times? How do you improve your heart rate variability? - How can you incorporate vagus nerve exercises into your school or classroom? - What stressors do parents bring into the school? How do you give parents vocabulary to help themselves and their children? - What are your primary "fire alarm" triggers, and how do you address them?
Application to classroom practice: (What processes or information will you use or incorporate in your classroom tomorrow?)	
Reflections: (Have any thoughts, feelings, or preconceived ideas shifted due to the chapter information?)	
Next steps: (What needs to be completed prior to the next meeting/session?)	

Chapter 6: A Brain-Based Approach to Parents/ Caregivers: The Emotional Dance of Parenting

- Parenting is an emotional issue and highly developed from parents' own experiences and stories
- Looking at parents from a brain-system approach and the emotional realities of parenting/caregiving

Goals for learning: (What are your professional goals or outcomes for this book study?)	
Focus questions and topics for the chapter: (Questions to answer as a group in response to the reading.)	▪ People parent the way they were parented or in response to the way they were parented. Which way do you parent? How do you see this impact the parents you work with? ▪ What bias indicators do you use to make judgments? How do these judgments impact your interaction with parents? ▪ Look at the Karpman triangle. Role-play with a colleague where they try to draw you into the triangle, but you are able to stay out of it. Was it easy? How do you help parents avoid becoming part of the triangle? ▪ Does your school have a strong community of support? If so, how can you help other buildings? If not, how can you strengthen the community of support?
Application to classroom practice: (What processes or information will you use or incorporate in your classroom tomorrow?)	
Reflections: (Have any thoughts, feelings, or preconceived ideas shifted due to the chapter information?)	
Next steps: (What needs to be completed prior to the next meeting/session?)	

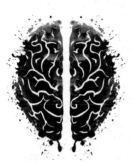

Appendix B

Integrated Unit for Algebra I: Bottled Water, Perspective-Taking, and Linear Equations

Developed by Michelle Zaludek

This unit requires the student to take on the perspective of a buyer. What would make a buyer want to buy this water? How do you look at the situation through someone else's eyes? What is their perspective? The ability to see the perspectives of others is the basis of all empathy.

Unit	Math Expertise	TEKS Readiness/Supporting Standards	
Linear equations	**Algebra** Student can manipulate and evaluate the formalized patterns, functions, and generalizations of mathematical thinking. Can manipulate, evaluate, and develop equations and representational systems. **Problem-Solving** Student can verbalize the questions around the problem. Can use multiple strategies. Can solve the problem more than one way and extrapolate additional possibilities. **Representations** Student uses multiple representational systems to model and interpret physical, social, and mathematical issues. Can represent at the conceptual, relationship, and concrete level, and verbally explain the representation.	**A.1 Foundations for Functions** The student understands that a function represents a dependence of one quantity on another and can be described in a variety of ways. A.1.A describe independent and dependent quantities in functional relationships A.1.B gather and record data and use data sets to determine functional relationships between quantities A.1.D represent relationships among quantities using concrete models, tables, graphs, diagrams, verbal descriptions, equations, and inequalities A.1.E interpret and make decisions, predictions, and critical judgments from functional relationships **A.3 Foundations for Functions** The student understands how algebra can be used to express generalizations and recognizes and uses the power of symbols to represent situations. A.3.A use symbols to represent unknowns and variables A.3.B look for patterns and represent generalizations algebraically **A.7 Linear Equations and Inequalities** The student formulates equations and inequalities based on linear functions, uses a variety of methods to solve them, and analyzes the solutions in terms of the situation. A.7.A analyze situations involving linear functions and formulate linear equations or inequalities to solve problems A.7.B investigate methods for solving linear equations and inequalities using concrete models, graphs, and the properties of equality, select a method, and solve the equations and inequalities	

	Project Idea Driving Questions	Skills and Learning Objectives	Assessments	Time
	Students will create an ad for a local bottled water company that highlights the benefits of locally manufactured and delivered water.	**Written Communication:** Students will create, solve, and graph equations that prove to the consumer buying local water has more economic benefits. **Oral Communication:** Students will give a 3–5 minute presentation explaining their product choices and how they relate to the expertise gained. **Collaboration:** Students will work in groups of 2–3 to research and interpret physical, social, and mathematical issues to complete their final product.	**Daily Reports:** Students will turn in daily progress reports outlining the work accomplished that day, as well as goals for the next class. **Project Rubric:** Students will present a summary of their project through their medium of choice and be evaluated by the teacher and their peers using an expertise rubric.	**1 week** **Introduction and Research:** 45 minutes **Content Knowledge Building:** 45 minutes **Presentation Prep:** 45 minutes **Presentations:** 45 minutes **Evaluation Summary:** 10 minutes

Dear Students,

Bottled water is one of the most successful commercial products of the last one hundred years. According to Peter Gelick, and expert in the industry, every second of every day in the United States, a thousand people buy a plastic bottle of water. Americans spent more money last year on bottled water than on soda. Water is big business, and we need your help.

We are a new, local bottled water company that needs your help in naming and marketing our product. We want to emphasize the benefits of being a local company in an ad, so we need you to research the cost of transporting non-local water into our community.

Good luck!

Project Checklist

☐ Name your product (5 points)

☐ Create a slogan that influences your target audience (5 points)

☐ Decide on an advertising medium (print, video, digital, other) (20 points)

☐ Research competition (20 points)

☐ Create, solve, and graph appropriate linear equations (50 points)

How will you present this information?
Options:

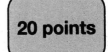

- Film a commercial

- Put your information in a slideshow

- Create a poster

- Other:

Your presentation must include:

- The name of your product

- A "catchy" slogan

- Cost of advertisement

- Cost of transportation

- The graph of your equations

Advertising Slogan

Water is free. Why should I buy it from you?

An advertising slogan is a quick phrase that helps consumers remember your product. You can use humor, but keep it simple, typically no more than one sentence.

5 points

Brainstorm:

_____

_____

_____

_____

_____

_____

Slogan:

_____

What's in a Name?

Pick a name and design a label that is exciting and memorable.

5 points

Name options (circle your favorite):

_____

_____

_____

_____

_____

_____

_____

Create a label: ⎯⎯⎯⎯⎯⎯→

Research Your Competition

1. Find three different water bottles. These are your competitors.

2. Look at the brand name, the slogan, and read any information written on the label.

3. Look for the source location on the label of the bottle.

4. Map the source location and find out the distance in miles from the source to you.

20 points

Water #1	Water #2	Water #3
Name	Name	Name
Slogan	Slogan	Slogan
Other information	Other information	Other information
Source	Source	Source
Distance from you in miles	Distance from you in miles	Distance from you in miles

Prove It

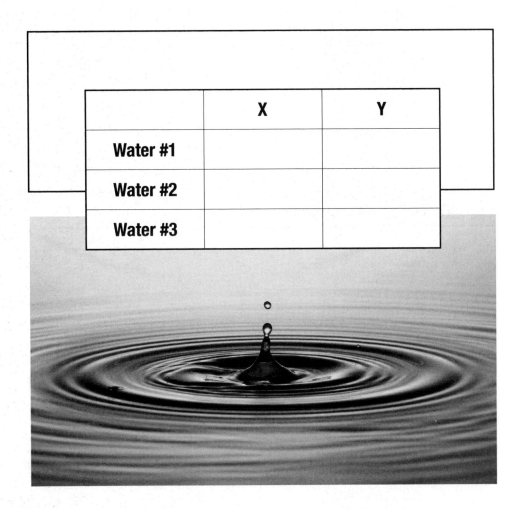

	X	Y
Water #1		
Water #2		
Water #3		

Prove It

- Set up and solve your equation for bottle #1

- Set up and solve your equation for bottle #2

- Set up and solve your equation for bottle #3

Prove It

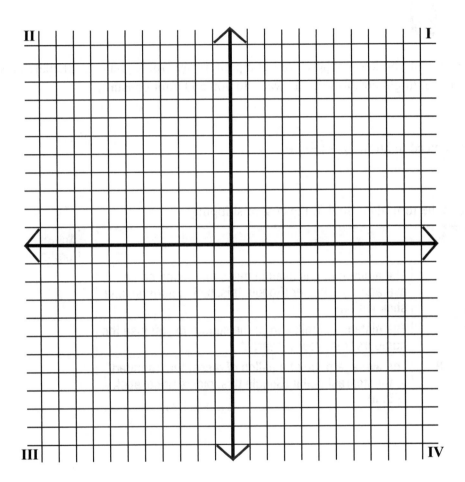

Prove It

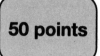

50 points

Now that you know where your competitors are from, you can calculate how much it might cost to ship the water to you and your consumers.

You need to know: $y = \left(\dfrac{x}{G}\right) P$

Use the formula to find Y, the cost of shipping.

		Actual Number
G	The amount of gas used in miles per gallon on an average 18-wheeler (Google this, pick a number, and stick with it)	
x	The distance in miles from the source to you (use the numbers from your research)	
P	The average price of a gallon of diesel fuel rounded to the nearest dollar (Google this, pick a price, stick with it)	

Skilled Mathematician Rubric

	Beginning	Developing	Capable	Expert
Problem-solving	Has no strategies to use to solve problems. No persistence. Does not understand what is being solved.	Has one strategy to use but gives up if that one does not work. Can identify what needs to be solved.	Has two or three strategies to use. Can set up the problem a couple of different ways. Can verbalize conceptually what the problem is seeking to know.	Can verbalize the questions around the problem. Can use multiple strategies. Can solve the problem more than one way. Extrapolates additional possibilities
Algebra	Has no idea that algebra helps to solve for the unknown. Can identify a few of the symbols and procedures. Basic equations are a challenge, and articulation of the problem is limited.	Uses the symbols and procedures. Can use some of the patterns and functions. Can verbalize some of the generalizations of algebra. Can articulate what the problem is trying to solve/find.	Uses the formalized patterns, functions, and generalizations of algebra. Can verbalize the thinking but is limited to the replication of what has been taught.	Can manipulate and evaluate the formalized patterns, functions, and generalizations of mathematical thinking. Can manipulate, evaluate, and develop equations and representational systems.
Representations (charts, drawings, pictures, concrete materials, tables, graphs, number and letter symbols, spreadsheets, music, time, symbols, equations, architecture, drafting, cooking, etc.)	Does not understand that math is a representational system of thinking. Uses numbers to count things, time to get to work/school, and space to live in but does not see these as related to math.	Knows a couple of representational systems but limited ability to verbally explain them or manipulate the data another way. Does know that math is representational.	Can use multiple representational systems but does not use them in an integrated way to express multiple findings— concepts, relationships, concrete realities, etc. Can articulate the representational nature of math and multiple applications.	Uses multiple representational systems to model and interpret physical, social, and mathematical issues. Can represent at the conceptual, relationship, and concrete level. Can verbally explain the representation as well.

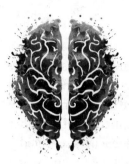

Appendix C

Why So Many Gifted Males Get Misidentified as Having ODD (Oppositional Defiant Disorder)

Why So Many Gifted Males Get Misidentified as Having ODD (Oppositional Defiant Disorder)

by Ruby K. Payne, Ph.D.

At a workshop I had a participant ask me why so many more males are now being identified as having ODD. Many times (but not always) these male students are not ODD but rather are gifted. If you are a gifted male from poverty or another marginalized group, you will more often be identified as ODD rather than gifted. When I was director of a gifted program, I had teachers repeatedly beg me not to teach "those gifted kids." When I asked why, I got the following responses: "They challenge me on everything. They are rude in the way they ask questions. If they don't like what I say, they will not do it. They argue about everything." Etc.

A friend of mine told me this story: She said, "If our fourth child had been our first child, he would have been our last child. I congratulated myself on being such a fabulous parent, and then I had our fourth child. Nothing worked. I still remember the day he refused to eat his peas. He was about two years old. I said to him, 'We will sit here until you eat your peas.' Four hours later, they were still sitting there. I thought, who is in charge here? It is not me."

What is the difference between a high achiever and a "gifted" student? There are generally two answers: It depends on where you fall on the standard deviation of intelligence (IQ) and on an additional set of characteristics.

Number One: Standard Deviation of Intelligence (IQ)

Standard Deviation of Intelligence (IQ)

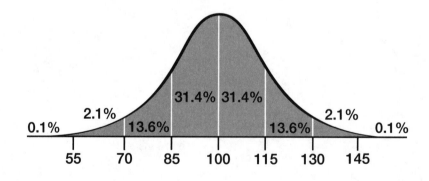

Many arguments can be made about the questions on IQ tests. IQ tests were developed to predict success in school. Since then, they have been equated with intelligence, which was never their purpose. But they are an indicator of the ability to learn academically and the speed with which you learn.

In standard deviation research, approximately 95% of the population falls two standard deviations (either way) from the norm.

"Giftedness" generally starts at an IQ of 130, which represents only 2.1% of the population. When you get to an IQ of 145, you are now three standard deviations from the norm, and only 0.01% of the population is there. When you get to an IQ of 160, you are four standard deviations from the norm. And IQ scores can go beyond that.

When a person is that far from the "norm" in intelligence, it is very difficult to "fit." You don't see the world the way other people do. Adults often seem "stupid," and why would you do what a "stupid" person tells you to do? A lot of the work in school is meaningless and seems like busywork. You often know the answer immediately. It is also hard for you to make and keep friends. Everyone is fairly boring. What you are interested in, they are not.

My late husband had three siblings with IQs over 150. To them, people in the normal range were "boring and stupid."

Number Two: A Set of Characteristics/Behaviors

The other identifier of those who are gifted is a set of characteristics that can show up as positives or negatives. In the following scale, you can see the characteristics identified in the research on a positive/negative continuum. Many of the characteristics of ODD show up on the negative side of the equation.

Slocumb–Payne Teacher Perception Inventory:
A Scale for Rating Superior Students from Diverse Backgrounds

Developed by Paul D. Slocumb, Ed.D. and Ruby K. Payne, Ph.D.

Student's name _____ Date _____

School _____ Grade _____ Age _____

Teacher/person completing this form _____

How long have you known this student? _____ years _____ months

Directions: This scale is designed to obtain a teacher's perception of a student's characteristics as a potentially gifted/talented student. This is not a recommendation form; it is a perception of a student within the context of a classroom or school. Since each classroom is as unique as the teacher conducting that classroom, one teacher's perception of a student may vary considerably from that of another.

The items are derived from the research literature dealing with characteristics of gifted and creative persons. A considerable number of individual differences can be found within any student population; therefore, the profiles are likely to vary a great deal. There is no right answer to any question.

Each descriptor item in each row should be read from the left and from the right, and then circle the applicable number that best describes your perception of the student as related to that descriptor. *You are to circle only one number in each row.* Each descriptor is designed to be "two sides of same coin." Persons completing this instrument may find it helpful to first read the descriptor on the left, then the one on the right, and then place a check mark beside the descriptor that best aligns with your perception of the student under consideration. Then, using that descriptor, circle the number that most closely describes your perception of the student in relation to the descriptor.

One descriptor item per row (either the one on the left or the right) is to be rated as follows:

    1 = Seldom or never

    2 = Occasionally

    3 = Frequently

    4 = Almost always

Perception of attributes	Seldom or never	Occasionally	Frequently	Almost always	Almost always	Frequently	Occasionally	Seldom or never	Perception of attributes
1. Curious about information; inquisitive; doesn't accept information at first glance; questions and pushes for more information	1	2	3	4	4	3	2	1	1. Obnoxious with questions; likes to "stump" people with hard questions; enjoys questions with "shock value"; questions authority; unwilling to follow rules
2. Stubborn; avoids tending to other things that need to be done just because student is not through with own priority	1	2	3	4	4	3	2	1	2. Sticks to task; gets job done; doesn't give up easily even when things are difficult
3. Finds it hard to wait for others; unwilling to do detail work; shows reluctance to do some assignments because the student already "knows" content or skill	1	2	3	4	4	3	2	1	3. Learns at faster rate than peer group; absorbs more with less practice; able to accelerate own learning; displays eagerness to do work
4. Understands subtleties of language in own primary language; uses language in powerful ways; displays unique sense of humor; able to use language to build personal relationships	1	2	3	4	4	3	2	1	4. "Smart mouth"; master at put-downs of others; uses humor in destructive manner; unable to relate to peers because own sense of humor isn't as sophisticated; class clown
5. Thirsts for knowledge; seeks answers to questions; motivated to do research to find answers to questions; likes rhetorical questions; curious about ideas	1	2	3	4	4	3	2	1	5. Shows little interest in what is to be learned; wants to pursue only those things that spark own curiosity; is more curious about people than events
6. Has difficulty completing tasks; unaware of deadlines; oblivious to those nearby; very focused on and committed to own priorities	1	2	3	4	4	3	2	1	6. Commits to long-range projects and tasks; focused; goal-oriented; strives to meet high standards
7. Loves ambiguity and dislikes being given specific directions and/or parameters; unable to be specific with other people who need specific direction; comes across as highly creative/inventive	1	2	3	4	4	3	2	1	7. Able and willing to ascertain and solve problems; does not need specific directions; may set own goals that surpass teacher's expectations
8. Deeply interested in many things; is good at many things; loves to learn new things	1	2	3	4	4	3	2	1	8. Unable to make decisions—or makes decisions quickly without regard for consequences; may hop from one thing to another without experiencing closure in anything; appears random
Subtotals of page 2									Total for this page

Perception of attributes	Seldom or never	Occasionally	Frequently	Almost always	Almost always	Frequently	Occasionally	Seldom or never	Perception of attributes
9. Develops high standards and expectations of self; self-starter who needs little supervision; has self-control	1	2	3	4	4	3	2	1	9. Perfectionist; nothing is ever good enough; can't finish something because it still isn't correct; may display low self-image about academic performance
10. Has trouble listening while others talk; interrupts others to point of rudeness; talks at inappropriate times; may be reluctant to write; very expressive in casual register	1	2	3	4	4	3	2	1	10. Excellent facility with language; can elaborate on thoughts and ideas; uses formal register when communicating with others
11. Highly developed social conscience; concern for social issues and problems; awareness of global issues; has internal locus of control	1	2	3	4	4	3	2	1	11. Overconcern for social problems and issues to extent that depression results; doomsday view of life; overwhelmed with despair in world/community; sees self as victim
12. Able to comprehend complex ideas and thoughts; able to learn advanced and more complex content	1	2	3	4	4	3	2	1	12. Out of touch with reality, day-to-day routines; bored by simpler things in life; unwilling or unable to abide by basic requirements and/or rules
13. Unwilling to learn facts to support generalizations; can be great "talker" but is unable to produce because work lacks substance	1	2	3	4	4	3	2	1	13. Sees patterns in things; can transfer learning to new situations; sees big picture; discovers new information; supports generalizations with facts/details
14. Makes connections; sees relationships between/among diverse ideas and events	1	2	3	4	4	3	2	1	14. Difficult to stay focused because of random thoughts/ideas; highly creative but perceived as "weird" by peers
15. Shows clever, unique responses to questions and problems; often responds with humor or offers "silly" response to questions	1	2	3	4	4	3	2	1	15. Generates large number of ideas or solutions to problems and questions; often offers unusual, unique, clever responses
16. Appreciates color; likes to doodle and draw; has affinity for graffiti	1	2	3	4	4	3	2	1	16. Sensitive to beauty; tunes in to aesthetic characteristics of things
17. Uninhibited in expressions of opinion; sometimes radical and spirited in disagreement; tenacious	1	2	3	4	4	3	2	1	17. Uninhibited in expressions of opinion; sometimes appears radical and disagreeable; may show anger when disagreeing with others
Subtotals of page 3									Total for this page

Perception of attributes	Seldom or never	Occasionally	Frequently	Almost always	Almost always	Frequently	Occasionally	Seldom or never	Perception of attributes
18. High risk-taker in academic endeavors; is adventurous and speculative in own thinking	1	2	3	4	4	3	2	1	18. Risk-taker; dares to break rules and then challenges authority when caught; unafraid to challenge others
19. Criticizes openly; unwilling to accept authoritarian rules and procedures; orally and openly condemns them; may irritate others	1	2	3	4	4	3	2	1	19. Criticizes constructively in socially acceptable manner; unwilling to accept authoritarian pronouncements without critical examinations

Subtotals of page 4									**Total for page 4**
									Total for page 3
									Total for page 2
									GRAND TOTAL

Source: *Removing the mask: How to identify and develop giftedness in students from poverty* (3rd ed.). Slocumb, P. D., Payne, R. K., & Williams, E. (2018).

According to Johns Hopkins Medicine, this is a list of ODD behaviors:

- "Having frequent temper tantrums
- Arguing a lot with adults
- Refusing to do what an adult asks
- Always questioning rules and refusing to follow rules
- Doing things to annoy or upset others, including adults
- Blaming others for the child's own misbehaviors or mistakes
- Being easily annoyed by others
- Often having an angry attitude
- Speaking harshly or unkindly
- Seeking revenge or being vindictive"

According to Wikipedia, "the following risks are listed in *The Social and Emotional Development of Gifted Children*:

- frustration, irritability, anxiety, tedium, and social isolation (p. 11)
- intense social isolation and stress among those with IQ greater than 160 (p. 14)

- difficulty making friends due to advanced concept of friendship, mostly among those less than age 10 (p. 23)

- demotivation, low self-esteem, and social rejection among the exceptionally gifted (p. 26)

- emotional awareness beyond their ability to control (p. 34)

- difficulty with peer relations proportional to their IQ (p. 35)

- loneliness, anxieties, phobias, interpersonal problems, fear of failure, and perfectionism (p. 43)

- underachievement for social acceptance (p. 64)

- lack of resilience reinforced by easy work and well-intentioned but misguided praise (p. 65)

- increasing perfectionism throughout school years among girls (p. 75)

- fear of failure and risk avoidance due to perfectionism (p. 75)

- depression among creatively gifted (p. 93)

"There is a cause-and-effect relationship between the unmet learning needs of gifted students and the above risks. 'Research indicates that many of the emotional and social difficulties gifted students experience disappear when their educational climates are adapted to their level and pace of learning.'

"Linda Kreger Silverman enumerates these additional risks:

- refusal to do routine, repetitive assignments

- inappropriate criticism of others

- lack of awareness of impact on others

- difficulty accepting criticism

- hiding talents to fit in with peers

- nonconformity and resistance to authority

- poor study habits

"Further, there exists anecdotal evidence of truancy problems with gifted children, who sometimes miss school because of disengagement, and worse, fear of bullying."

As you can see, many of the characteristics of gifted at-risk students are very similar to those of students with ODD.

A Disproportionate Number of Gifted Students Drop Out or Underperform

The Wikipedia article on gifted at-risk students concludes: "Lastly, meta-analysis from the paper 'Gifted Students Who Drop Out—Who and Why: A Meta-Analytical Review of the Literature' by Kaskaloglu shows two key points. First, 4.5% of high school dropouts are gifted, and they leave school in part because of school-related issues. To understand the dropout rate, one must consider that the study cited indicates the percentage of children who both dropped out and who scored above 130 on an IQ test. One would expect a very small percentage of such children to drop out, given the ease with which they can excel in school. To expect more than one in ten would be hard to justify. Therefore, with only 2.27% of people scoring above 130 on IQ tests, to expect greater than 0.227% of dropouts to be gifted would be ostensibly far-fetched. Unfortunately, the actual percentage is closer to 20 times that. According to Achievement Trap, this problem is even more pronounced among economically disadvantaged children."

Before you label a male student as ODD, please do the following:

1. Give an IQ test. If the student is from poverty, do the environmental assessment that is in the book *Removing the Mask: How to Identify and Develop Giftedness in Students from Poverty*.

2. Do the rating scale in the teacher perception inventory. How many of the gifted behaviors are there? Particularly on the "negative" side of the scale?

Strategies That Get Much Better Results from Gifted Males

1. Everything must involve a choice. Gifted males do not respond well to mandates.

2. Everything will involve a discussion. Count on it. If you use phrases like "because I said so," expect outright refusal. Encourage them to research the issue being discussed.

3. Do not use psychological control (comments about who they are or who they should be); instead, use behavioral control (comments about boundaries, laws, and guidelines).

4. Gifted males do not respond well to negative reinforcers (taking things away, etc.). They will respond much better to positive reinforcers (working for things they want).

5. Gifted males will push the boundaries on everything. Decide which battles you have to fight and which ones you do not. Otherwise, you will be fighting about everything.

6. Understand that gifted students are generally two grade levels above their peers academically but two years behind their peers emotionally. Because they are so acutely aware of everything, they have an increased sensitivity.

7. If they believe you have violated something they consider to be an ethical issue, they will be unforgiving.

Before you decide a male has ODD, please do more research. By nurturing giftedness rather than suspecting a disorder, you may allow an unbelievable talent to develop.

Appendix C References

Gifted At-Risk. (2020). Wikipedia. https://en.wikipedia.org/wiki/Gifted_At-Risk

Johns Hopkins Medicine. (2020). Oppositional defiant disorder (ODD) in children. https://www.hopkinsmedicine.org/health/conditions-and-diseases/oppositional-defiant-disorder

Slocumb, P. D., Payne, R. K., & Williams, E. (2018). *Removing the mask: How to identify and develop giftedness in students from poverty* (3rd ed.). aha! Process

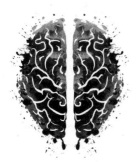

Bibliography

Adams, K. M. (2011). *Silently seduced: When parents make their children partners.* Health Communications.

Adelson, S., Bell, R., Graff, A., Goldenberg, D., Haase, E., Downey, J., & Friedman, R. C. (2012). Toward a definition of 'hypersexuality' in children and adolescents. *Psychodynamic Psychiatry, 40*(3), 419–435. https://doi.org/10.1521/pdps.2012.40.3.481

Amen, D. G. (2013). *Unleash the power of the female brain: Supercharging yours for better health, energy, mood, focus, and sex.* Harmony Books.

Amen, D. G. (2015). *Change your brain, change your life: The breakthrough program for conquering anxiety, depression, obsessiveness, lack of focus, anger, and memory problems.* Harmony Books.

Arain, M., Haque, M., Johal, L., Mathur, P., Nel, W., Rais, A., Sandhu, R., & Sharma, S. (2013). Maturation of the adolescent brain. *Neuropsychiatric Disease and Treatment, 9,* 449–461. https://doi.org/10.2147/NDT.S39776

Arnsten, A. (2009). Stress signalling pathways that impair prefrontal cortex structure and function. *National Review of Neuroscience, 10,* 410–422. https://doi.org/10.1038/nrn2648

Association of American Educators. (n.d.). Character education programs. https://www.aaeteachers.org/index.php/character-education-programs

Beck, J. (n.d.). How pornography affects teenagers [and children]. EverAccountable. https://everaccountable.com/blog/how-pornography-affects-teenagers-and-children

Berger, K. S. (2009). *Invitation to the life span.* Macmillan.

Berger, K. S. (2014). *The developing person through the life span* (9th ed.). Worth.

Blakemore, S.-J. (2018). *Inventing ourselves: The secret life of the teenage brain.* BBS Public Affairs.

Brookshire, B. (2016, July 15). Hormone affects how teens' brains control emotions. Science News for Students. https://www.sciencenewsforstudents.org/article/hormone-affects-how-teens-brains-control-emotions

Burns, G. W. (2005). *101 healing stories for kids and teens: Using metaphors in therapy.* John Wiley and Sons.

Carran, L. A. (2013). *101 trauma-informed interventions: Activities, exercises, and assignments to move the client and therapy forward.* Premier.

Carse, J. P. (1986). *Finite and infinite games: A vision of life as play and possibility.* Simon & Schuster.

Cassetta, G., & Wilson, M. (2019, September 24). Recognizing schools' institutional bias. Heinemann Blog. https://blog.heinemann.com/recognizing-schools-institutional-bias

Chhetry, B. T., Hezghia, A., Miller, J. M., Lee, S., Rubin-Falcone, H., Cooper, T. B., … & Sublette, M. E. (2016). Omega-3 polyunsaturated fatty acid supplementation and white matter changes in major depression. *Journal of Psychiatric Research, 75,* 65–74. https://doi.org/10.1016/j.jpsychires.2015.12.007

Childre, D. L., & Martin, H., with Beech, D. (2000). *The HeartMath solution: The Institute of HeartMath's revolutionary program for engaging the power of the heart's intelligence.* HarperOne.

Choudhury, S., Blakemore, S.-J., & Charman, T. (2006). Social cognitive development during adolescence. *Social Cognitive and Affective Neuroscience, 1*(3), 165–174. http://doi.org/10.1093/scan/nsl024

Church, D. (2018). *Mind to matter: The astonishing science of how your brain creates material reality.* Hay House.

Clark, R. C. (2008). *Building expertise: Cognitive methods for training and performance.* Pfeiffer.

Clear, J. (2018). *Atomic habits: An easy and proven way to build good habits and break bad ones.* Avery.

Cornah, D. (2006). The impact of spirituality on mental health: A review of the literature. Mental Health Foundation. https://www.mentalhealth.org.uk/sites/default/files/impact-spirituality.pdf

Cron, I. M., & Stabile, S. (2016). *The road back to you: An enneagram journey to self-discovery.* IVP Books.

Dalio, R. (2017). *Principles: Life and work.* Simon & Schuster.

Dana, D. (2018). *The polyvagal theory in therapy: Engaging the rhythm of regulation.* W. W. Norton.

Delahooke, M. (2019). *Beyond behaviors: Using brain science and compassion to understand and solve children's behavioral challenges.* PESI.

Devitt, M. (2018, May 21). Research finds acupuncture effective for chronic pain. American Academy of Family Physicians. https://www.aafp.org/news/health-of-the-public/20180521acupuncture.html

Duncombe, J. (2019, December 12). Human brains have tiny bits of magnetic material. *Eos.* https://eos.org/articles/human-brains-have-tiny-bits-of-magnetic-material

Eden, D., with Dahlin, D. (2012). *The little book of energy medicine.* Jeremy P. Tarcher.

Eisler, M. (2018, June 29). What's the difference between meditation and mindfulness? The Chopra Institute. https://chopra.com/articles/whats-the-difference-between-meditation-and-mindfulness

El Puente Project. (2009). Helping Latino high school youth make something of themselves: Lessons from El Puente. https://issuu.com/latinoyouthcollective/docs/bestpracticebrief

Elite HRV. (n.d.). Normative elite HRV scores by age and gender. https://elitehrv.com/normal-heart-rate-variability-age-gender

Elkind, D. (1967). Egocentrism in adolescence. *Child Development, 38,* 1025–1034.

Feinstein, D., Eden, D., & Craig, G. (2005). *The promise of energy psychology.* Jeremy P. Tarcher.

Fight the New Drug. (n.d.). Love is natural. Porn is produced. https://fightthenewdrug.org/media/love-is-natural-porn-is-produced/

Fight the New Drug. (2017). *Brain heart world* [documentary series]. https://brainheartworld.org

Fight the New Drug. (2017, August 23). How porn affects the brain like a drug. https://fightthenewdrug.org/how-porn-affects-the-brain-like-a-drug

Fight the New Drug. (2018, September 18). How watching porn can mess with your brain—literally. https://fightthenewdrug.org/how-porn-can-mess-with-your-brain

Fight the New Drug. (2019, May 30). Can watching porn actually be healthy for you? https://fightthenewdrug.org/is-porn-healthy

Forward, S. (1997). *Emotional blackmail: When the people in your life use fear, obligation, and guilt to manipulate you.* HarperCollins.

Friederichs, A. (2018, spring). How the adult brain learns: The importance of creating enriched environments when teaching. *Unbound.* https://unbound.upcea.edu/innovation/contemporary-learners/how-the-adult-brain-learns-the-importance-of-creating-enriched-environments-when-teaching/

Galbraith, J. (1985). The eight great gripes of gifted kids: Responding to special needs. *Roeper Review, 8,* 15–18.

Gibson, L. C. (2015). *Adult children of emotionally immature parents: How to heal from distant, rejecting, or self-involved parents.* New Harbinger.

Giedd, J. N. (2008). The teen brain: Insights from neuroimaging. *Journal of Adolescent Health, 42*(4), 335–343. https://doi.org/10.1016/j.jadohealth.2008.01.007

Giedd, J. N. (2012). The digital revolution and adolescent brain evolution. *Journal of Adolescent Health, 51*(2), 101–105. https://doi.org/10.1016/j.jadohealth.2012.06.002

Gullo, G. L., Capatosto, K., & Staats, C. (2018). *Implicit bias in schools: A practitioner's guide.* Routledge.

Habib, N. (2019). *Activate your vagus nerve.* Ulysses Press.

Hammel, S. (2019). *Handbook of therapeutic storytelling.* Routledge.

Hand, K. (2017). *Magic words and language patterns.* ReMind.

HeartMath Institute. (n.d.). Coherence. https://www.heartmath.org/research/science-of-the-heart/coherence

HeartMath Institute. (n.d.). Energetic communication. https://www.heartmath.org/research/science-of-the-heart/energetic-communication

HeartMath Institute. (n.d.). Heart rate variability: An indicator of self-regulatory capacity, autonomic function and health. https://www.heartmath.org/research/science-of-the-heart/heart-rate-variability/

HeartMath Institute. (n.d.). Heart-brain communication. https://www.heartmath.org/research/science-of-the-heart/heart-brain-communication/

How Youth Learn. (2013). The teenage brain: Research highlights. https://www.howyouthlearn.org/research_teenagebrain.html

Jain, S., Hammerschlag, R., Mills, P., Cohen, L., Krieger, R., Vieten, C., & Lutgendorf, S. (2015). Clinical studies of biofield therapies: Summary, methodological challenges, and recommendations. *Global advances in health and medicine, 4*(Suppl), 58–66. https://doi.org/10.7453/gahmj.2015.034.suppl

Jewell, T. (2018, September 19). How long does it take for sperm to regenerate? What to expect. Healthline. https://www.healthline.com/health/mens-health/how-long-does-it-take-for-sperm-to-regenerate

Jose, J. M. (2016, September 12). Teaching morality: Kohlberg's theory of moral development. Angles and Superheroes. https://angelsandsuperheroes.com/2016/09/12/teaching-morality-kohlbergs-theory-of-moral-development/

Kelly, G. (2017, September 11): The scary effects of pornography: How the 21st century's acute addiction is rewiring our brains. *The Telegraph.* https://www.telegraph.co.uk/men/thinking-man/scary-effects-pornography-21st-centurys-accute-addiction-rewiring

Kotler, S., & Wheal, J. (2017). *Stealing fire: How Silicon Valley, the Navy SEALS, and maverick scientists are revolutionizing the way we live and work.* Dey Street Books.

Kramer, P., & Bressan, P. (2017). Our (mother's) mitochondria and our mind. *Perspectives on Psychological Science, 13*(1), 88–100. https://doi.org/10.1177/1745691617718356

Kurtus, R. (2012, March 18). Noise cancellation. Ron Kurtus' School for Champions. http://www.school-for-champions.com/science/noise_cancellation. htm#.XhiZi_xOlEZ

Kurtus, R. (2013, October 2013). Beat frequencies in sound. Ron Kurtus' School for Champions. http://www.school-for-champions.com/science/sound_beat_ frequencies.htm#.XhdQ7fxOlEY

Ledoux, J., & Gorman, J. M. (2002). A call to action: Overcoming anxiety through active coping. *American Journal of Psychiatry 158*(12), 1953–1955. https://doi. org/10.1176/appi.ajp.158.12.1953

Lipton, B. (2013). *The honeymoon effect: The science of creating heaven on earth.* Hay House.

Love, S. (2017, April 28). How prayer and meditation changes your brain. *Vice.* https://www.vice.com/en_us/article/nzpk9w/how-prayer-and-meditation-changes-your-brain

Loyd, A. (n.d.). *The success codes: Unlocking the cellular secrets of success* [digital manual]. Author.

Loyd, A. (n.d.). *The truth technique* [digital manual]. Author.

Loyd, A. (2019). *The memory code: The 10-minute solution for healing your life through memory engineering.* Grand Central.

Loyd, A., with Johnson, B. (2013). *The healing code: 6 minutes to heal the source of your health, success, or relationship issue.* Grand Central Life & Style.

MacLaughlin, K. (n.d.). 7 effects of screen time on kids' brain development. Zift Parent Portal. https://wezift.com/parent-portal/blog/7-effects-of-screen-time-on-kids-brain-development

Martinez, M. (2016). *The mindbody code: How to change the beliefs that limit your health, longevity, and success.* Sounds True.

Mathieu, F. (2012). *The compassion fatigue workbook: Creative tools for transforming compassion fatigue and vicarious traumatization.* Routledge.

Mathis, M. (n.d.). 5 things parents wish teachers knew for conferences. TeachHub. https://www.teachhub.com/5-things-parents-wish-teachers-knew-parent-teacher-conferences

McLean, K. C. (2016). *The coauthored self: Family stories and the construction of personal identity.* Oxford University Press.

Miller, G. (2010, May). How our brains make memories. *Smithsonian Magazine.* https://www.smithsonianmag.com/science-nature/how-our-brains-make-memories-14466850

Myss, C. (1998). *Why people don't heal and how they can.* Harmony.

National Institute on Drug Abuse. (2016, February). Understanding drug abuse and addiction: What science says. https://www.drugabuse.gov/publications/teaching-packets/understanding-drug-abuse-addiction/section-i/4-reward-pathway

Navarro, J. (2008). *What every body is saying: An ex-FBI agent's guide to speed-reading people.* HarperCollins.

Neff, K. (2011). *Self-compassion: The proven power of being kind to yourself.* HarperCollins.

Newberg, A. B. (2014). The neuroscientific study of spiritual practices. *Frontiers in Psychology, 5*(215). https://doi.org/10.3389/fpsyg.2014.00215

Newberg, A. B., & Waldman, M. R. (2012). *Words can change your brain: 12 conversation strategies to build trust, resolve conflict, and increase intimacy.* Plume.

Overview: Institutional bias. (2020). Oxford Reference. https://www.oxfordreference.com/view/10.1093/oi/authority.20110803100005347?rskey=jWjRio&result=2

Panda, S. (2018). *The circadian code: Lose weight, supercharge your energy, and transform your health from morning to midnight.* Rodale Books.

Payne, R. K. (2013). *Achievement for all: Keys to educating middle grades students in poverty.* Association for Middle Level Education.

Payne, R. K. (2018). *Emotional poverty in all demographics: How to reduce anger, anxiety, and violence in the classroom.* aha! Process.

Payne, R. K. (2019, March 7). Leadership: Three emotional 'mindtraps.' Linkedin. https://www.linkedin.com/pulse/leadership-three-emotional-mindtraps-ruby-k-payne-ph-d-

Payne, R. K., & O'Neill-Baker, E. (2015). *How much of yourself do you own? A process for building your emotional resources.* aha! Process.

PBS. (2002, January 31). Inside the teenage brain. *Frontline.* https://www.pbs.org/wgbh/frontline/film/inside-the-teenage-brain/

PBS. (2014). Interview: Jay Giedd. *Frontline.* https://www.pbs.org/wgbh/pages/frontline/shows/teenbrain/interviews/giedd.html

Pederson, L., with Pederson, C. S. (2017). *The expanded dialectical behavior therapy skills training manual: DBT for self-help and individual & group treatment settings.* Premier.

Pickhardt, C. E. (2016, September 5). Puberty and preoccupation with personal appearance. *Psychology Today.* https://www.psychologytoday.com/us/blog/surviving-your-childs-adolescence/201609/puberty-and-preoccupation-personal-appearance

Pietrangelo, A. (2014, April 21). The effects of testosterone on the body. *Healthline.* https://www.healthline.com/health/low-testosterone/effects-on-body#1

Pinker, S. (2019, March 27). Women have younger brains than men. *The Wall Street Journal.* https://www.wsj.com/articles/women-have-younger-brains-than-men-11553708268

Pittman, C. M., & Karle, E. (2015). *Rewire your anxious brain: How to use the neuroscience of fear to end anxiety, panic, and worry.* New Harbinger.

Porges, S. (2017). *The pocket guide to the polyvagal theory: The transformative power of feeling safe.* W. W. Norton.

Radcliffe, S. (2018, December 19). Is screen time altering the brains of children? *Healthline.* https://www.healthline.com/health-news/how-does-screen-time-affect-kids-brains

Raising Children Network. (2017, November 12). Brain development: Teenagers. https://raisingchildren.net.au/pre-teens/development/understanding-your-pre-teen/brain-development-teens

Raising Children Network. (2019). How to stop cyberbullying. https://raisingchildren.net.au/__data/assets/pdf_file/0031/34888/How-to-stop cyberbullying-PIP.pdf

Rajmohan, V., & Mohandas, E. (2007). Mirror neuron system. *Indian Journal of Psychiatry, 49*(1), 66–69. https://doi.org/10.4103/0019-5545.31522

Rizzolatti, G. & Sinigaglia, C. (2006). *Mirrors in the brain: How our minds share actions and emotions* (F. Anderson, Trans.). Oxford University Press.

Roeper, A. (1988). Should educators of the gifted and talented be more concerned with world issues? *Roeper Review, 11,* 12–13.

Rosenberg, S. (2017). *Accessing the healing power of the vagus nerve: Self-help exercises for anxiety, depression, trauma, and autism.* North Atlantic Books.

Rothschild, B. (2017). *The body remembers, volume 2: Revolutionizing trauma treatment.* W. W. Norton.

Rubik, B., Muehsam, D., Hammerschlag, R., & Jain, S. (2015). Biofield science and healing: History, terminology, and concepts. *Global advances in health and medicine, 4*(Suppl), 8–14. https://doi.org/10.7453/gahmj.2015.038.suppl

Ruder, G. B. (n.d.). Screen time and the brain. On the Brain: The Harvard Mahoney Neuroscience Institute Letter. https://neuro.hms.harvard.edu/harvard-mahoney-neuroscience-institute/brain-newsletter/and-brain-series/screen-time-and-brain

Rukeyser, M. (n.d.). The speed of darkness. Poetry Foundation. https://www.poetryfoundation.org/poems/56287/the-speed-of-darkness

Schulte, B. (2015, May 26). Harvard neuroscientist: Meditation not only reduces stress, here's how it changes your brain. *The Washington Post.* https://www.washingtonpost.com/news/inspired-life/wp/2015/05/26/harvard-neuroscientist-meditation-not-only-reduces-stress-it-literally-changes-your-brain

ScienceDirect. (n.d.). Social cognition. https://www.sciencedirect.com/topics/neuroscience/social-cognition

Siddiqui, S. V., Chatterjee, U., Kumar, D., Siddiqui, A., & Goyal, N. (2008). Neuropsychology of prefrontal cortex. *Indian Journal of Psychiatry, 50*(3), 202–208. https://doi.org/10.4103/0019-5545.43634

Siegel, D. J. (2010). *Mindsight: The new science of personal transformation.* Bantam.

Silverman, L. K. (1993). Social development, leadership, and gender issues. In L. K. Silverman (Ed.), *Counseling the gifted and talented* (pp. 291–327). Love Publishing.

Silverman, L. K. (1994). The moral sensitivity of gifted children and the evolution of society. *Roeper Review, 17,* 110–116.

Sipherd, R. (2018, February 22). The third-leading cause of death in U.S. most doctors don't want you to know about. CNBC. https://www.cnbc.com/2018/02/22/medical-errors-third-leading-cause-of-death-in-america.html

Solnit, R. (2013). *The faraway nearby.* Penguin.

Srebro, T. (2017, September 14). Doing good can make you feel good, study on volunteerism finds. VolunteerMatch. https://blogs.volunteermatch.org/volunteeringiscsr/2017/09/14/doing-good-can-make-you-feel-good-study-on-volunteerism-finds/

Stoddard, J., & Afari, N. (2014). *The big book of ACT metaphors.* New Harbinger.

Stosny, S. (1995). *Treating attachment abuse: A compassionate approach.* Springer.

Stosny, S. (2016). S*oar above: How to use the most profound part of your brain under any kind of stress.* Health Communications.

Stosny, S. (2018). *Empowered love: Use your brain to be your best self and create your ideal relationship.* IXIA Press.

Targonskaya, A. (2019, October 25). How many eggs do women have? *Flo.* https://flo.health/getting-pregnant/trying-to-conceive/fertility/how-many-eggs-do-women-have

Twerski, A.J. (1997). *Addictive thinking: Understanding self-deception.* Hazelden.

U.S. Department of Health and Human Services, Office of Population Affairs. (n.d.). Adolescent development explained. https://www.hhs.gov/ash/oah/adolescent-development/explained

Walker, M. (2017). *Why we sleep: Unlocking the power of sleep and dreams.* Scribner.

Warren, R. (2019, June 12). 10 signs you're emotionally exhausted. PastorRick. https://pastorrick.com/10-signs-youre-emotionally-exhausted/

Wennesheimer, H. M. (2017). Evaluating factors used by mental health professionals to access juvenile adjudicative competency. Walden University ScholarWorks. https://pdfs.semanticscholar.org/fe7f/40d1f81a128fcc923607e817ac2c8d06bd97.pdf

Wikipedia. (n.d.). Sex and gender distinction. https://en.wikipedia.org/wiki/Sex_and_gender_distinction

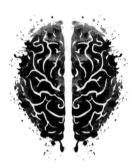

Index

[Page numbers in *italics* refer to tables or illustrations.]

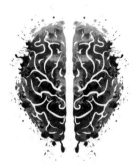

About the Author

Ruby K. Payne, Ph.D. is CEO and founder of aha! Process and an author, speaker, publisher, and career educator. She is a leading expert on the mindsets of economic class and on crossing socioeconomic lines in education and work. Payne is recognized internationally for her foundational and award-winning book, *A Framework for Understanding Poverty,* now in its sixth edition, which has sold more than 1.8 million copies. Payne has helped students and adults of all economic backgrounds achieve academic, professional, and personal success.

Payne's expertise stems from more than 30 years of experience in public schools. She has traveled extensively and has presented her work throughout North America and in Europe, Australia, China, and India. She has spoken to more than 2 million educators and trained more than 7,000 trainers to do her work. Her speaking engagements have included EARCOS (East Asia Regional Council of Schools) in Malaysia, National Association of School Boards, Central States Bankers Conference, Federal Reserve Board of Governors, Beijing Institute of Education, Harvard Summer Institute for Principals, as well as thousands of individual school districts and campuses.

Payne has written or coauthored more than a dozen books. Recent publications are the popular and award-winning *Emotional Poverty in All Demographics,* the digital (and free) *Before You Quit Teaching,* which won the Independent Publisher Book Awards gold medal for an adult informational ebook, the revised edition of *Research-Based Strategies: Narrowing the Achievement Gap for Under-Resourced Students* (coauthored with Bethanie H. Tucker, Ed.D.), which won the Independent Publisher Book Awards bronze educational resource award, *How Much of Yourself Do You Own? A Process for Building Your Emotional Resources* (coauthored with Emilia O'Neill-Baker, Ph.D.), and the third revised edition of *Removing the Mask: How to Identify and Develop Giftedness in Students from Poverty* (coauthored with Paul D. Slocumb, Ed.D. and Ellen Williams, Ed.D.). The previous edition of *Removing the Mask* won a gold medal from the Independent Publisher Book Awards.

Another major publication is *Bridges Out of Poverty* (coauthored with Philip E. DeVol and Terie Dreussi-Smith), which offers strategies for building sustainable communities. Payne's mission of raising student achievement and overcoming poverty has become a cornerstone for school improvement efforts undertaken by educational districts and Bridges communities across the United States.

Other publications include *Under-Resourced Learners: 8 Strategies to Boost Student Achievement, Hidden Rules of Class at Work* (coauthored with Don Krabill), *School Improvement: 9 Systemic Processes to Raise Achievement* (coauthored with Donna Magee, Ed.D.), *Crossing the Tracks for Love: What to Do When You and Your Partner Grew Up in Different Worlds, Living on a Tightrope: A Survival Handbook for Principals* (coauthored with William Sommers, Ph.D.), *What Every Church Member Should Know About Poverty* (coauthored with Bill Ehlig), *Achievement for All: Keys to Educating Middle Grades Students in Poverty* (published by the Association for Middle Level Education), and *Boys in Poverty: A Framework for Understanding Dropout* (coauthored with Paul D. Slocumb, Ed.D. and published by Solution Tree Press), which received the Distinguished Achievement Award from the Association of Educational Publishers in the professional development category.

Payne received a bachelor's degree from Goshen College, a Master's Degree in English Literature from Western Michigan University, and her Ph.D. in Educational Leadership and Policy from Loyola University Chicago.

 **Connect with us at ahaprocess.com**

- Visit ahaprocess.com for free resources: articles, video clips, and success stories from practitioners—and read our aha! Moments blog!

- Sign up for our latest LIVE online workshop offerings at ahaprocess.com/events:
  - Emotional Poverty workshop AND Trainer Certification
  - Bridges Across Every Divide
  - Getting Ahead in a Just-Gettin'-By World
  - Bridges Out of Poverty workshop AND Trainer Certification
  - Tactical Communication
  - Research-Based Strategies

- Register for on-demand workshops at ahaprocess.com/on-demand

- If you like *Emotional Poverty, Volume 2,* check out these publications:
  - *Emotional Poverty in All Demographics: How to Reduce Anger, Anxiety, and Violence in the Classroom* (Payne)
  - *A Framework for Understanding Poverty: A Cognitive Approach, 6th Edition* (Payne)
  - *Research-Based Strategies: Narrowing the Achievement Gap for Under-Resourced Students* (Payne & Tucker)
  - *Bridges Across Every Divide: Policy and Practices to Reduce Poverty and Build Communities* (DeVol & Krebs)
  - *Workplace Stability: Creating Conditions That Lead to Retention, Productivity, and Engagement in Entry-Level Workers* (Weirich)
  - *Tactical Communication, 3rd Edition: Tools for First Responders* (Pfarr)

- Connect with us on Facebook, Twitter, and Instagram—and watch our YouTube channel

For a complete listing of products, please visit ahaprocess.com

Join us on Facebook
facebook.com/rubypayne
facebook.com/bridgesoutofpoverty

Twitter
@ahaprocess
#AddressPoverty
#BridgesOutofPoverty

Subscribe to our YouTube channel
youtube.com/ahaprocess

Read our blog
ahaprocess.com/blog

Instagram
@ahaprocess